Sing for Your Supper

Yvonne Michie Horn

Sing for

EARNING YOUR

Harcourt Brace Jovanovic

Your Supper,

LIVING AS A SINGER

New York and London

Library of Congress Cataloging in Publication Data

Horn, Yvonne Michie.
Sing for your supper.

SUMMARY: Interviews 13 young singers who discuss
their climb to success in a wide range of musical
careers including teacher, church musician, studio
singer, theater performer, songwriter-singer, and jazz
stylist.
1. Singing—Juvenile literature. 2. Singing.
3. Music—Vocational guidance—Juvenile literature.
4. Music—Vocational guidance. [1. Singing. 2. Music
—Vocational guidance. 3. Vocational guidance.
4. Singers] I. Title.
ML3930.A2H67   784'.023   79–87519
ISBN 0–15–274959–4

First edition
B C D E

To the three on the piano bench . . .

Jon, Jennifer, and Joanne

Contents

Author's Note

Thousands of young people love to sing. All over the country, high school music and drama departments are filled to capacity with teen-agers who find great enjoyment using their voices.

But the fact is that most do not dare consider the possibility that they might pursue singing as a career. They either have no idea of the varied job possibilities or are intimidated by the "show biz" mysteries of the glamour jobs they have heard of.

It's sad to think of the super talents discouraged—there is always room at the top. And what of those with modest talents to share? There are places for them in the singing world, too, if they know what possibilities exist and how to go about preparing for them.

Sing for Your Supper is for and about young singers. It was written because, not so many years ago, I was a fledgling myself, singing for my supper. How I wish this book had been around then for me to read! It would have told me that there were more ways for me to earn my living with a song than I'd dreamed possible. I would have heard first hand from young singers, working full time at their careers, what the business is really like. How much I would have learned from their experiences!

The singers you will meet may or may not be known to you. All are young musicians who, in the eyes of those in the know in the music world, have the potential to be tops in their professions. The future will tell.

So, for you who love to sing, here is the book I'd like to have read.

Sing for Your Supper

1

A Career as a Singer

Applause crescendoes from the audience. Linda Roark acknowledges the ovation with a deep bow that almost takes her to her knees. "Bravo! Bravo!" An armful of roses appears over the footlights. Linda takes a final sweeping bow and exits, stage right, before the applause begins to subside.

"Gino Vannelli Creates Excitement," says the headline in a Chicago newspaper. But hours before the critic's review hit the stands, Gino and his brothers had packed up their keyboards and were off to another city, another stage, for another one-nighter where fans scream with recognition when Gino sings the first words of his hit single, "People Gotta Move."

"Verlin Sandles in Charge . . . 8 P.M.," reads the billboard on the wall outside the Macedonia Baptist Church. Inside, dressed in a floor-length print dress, hands clasped simply in front of her, Verlin's rich voice meanders effortlessly through the gospel songs she loves. "This world is not my home, I'm only a stranger here," she sings. "Amen! Praise the Lord!" responds the congregation.

Linda, Gino, and Verlin are only three of the young professional singers you will meet in this book. Like the others you will read about in the pages to come, they have studied, polished their talents, perfected their techniques, and have carved out a niche for themselves in the music world.

In every city and town in the United States, there are young people who love to sing, whose voices give enjoyment to others, who cannot imagine a day complete without singing a song. Perhaps you are one of them. And if you are like most, you have been given the distinct impression that singers come from somewhere else, that their careers are mysteriously God-given; that singing will be only a sideline in your life, that there is little possibility that you can sing for your supper. But this is not true.

Internationally famous stars come from somewhere. Why not from your town? For instance, you will read about baritone Lenus Carlson, who is now well on his way to worldwide fame. Lenus spent the first eighteen years of his life in a North Dakota community whose population dropped to ninety-nine when Lenus left home to try his musical wings. How great would be the music world's loss if Lenus had put his talent and ability aside in the belief that stars come from only a few specially chosen, cosmopolitan, and culturally sophisticated big cities.

"I love to sing, but my voice isn't *all that* spectacular," you may quite truthfully say. No matter that audiences will never pelt you with roses. You can still sing for your supper. There are more careers for singers than most people imagine—satisfying careers that may match perfectly your unique talents and interests. Are you an excellent musician, a quick sight-reader? Like Melissa Mackay, plan to make your living as a studio singer who creates commercials for radio and television, adds a backup voice behind a big-name artist, or "puts down" demonstration records for music publishing companies. Does your voice mirror the concern you feel for others? Like Genola Spoonhour, you may find satisfaction in the relatively new career of music therapy. Do you enjoy expressing your thoughts and feelings through your own lyrics and tunes? As Kim Carnes and Eddie Rabbitt know, the pop field has never been more receptive to singers who also write their own material.

This book will show you the way through informal conversations with young singers. The book asks what they did, why, when; how they feel about their work and what they intend to do next; how they keep their career as a singer on an upward scale.

As you look through the keyhole into the lives of these professional singers, you will find that there are certain guidelines for success, guidelines against which you can measure your own potential and pattern your own pathway toward a career.

You will find that the following seven ingredients are indispensable for success. Some careers demand more of one ingredient than another, but whether you teach small children or stride out on stage in satin jeans carrying a guitar, all must be present to some degree.

1. The ability to sing in tune
2. A sense of rhythm
3. A quick mind and a good memory
4. A good musical education
5. Good health and stamina
6. Tenacity
7. Talent

Let's take them one by one.

The ability to sing in tune. Obviously a singer with a tin ear has as many strikes against him or her as a mountain climber who has left his rope and spiked boots home. It's going to take a lot of scrambling to get to the top. No matter how rich the vocal timbre, how expressively sung the song, it's guaranteed to leave the audience cringing if the notes come out less than dead center. Some cases of faulty pitch can be corrected, but it takes great concentration and laborious effort to do so. A singer with a pitch problem is starting miles behind those who correctly voice their songs. Put one large check on the side of success if you never sing a note out of tune.

A sense of rhythm. This means more than the ability to tap your toe in time to the music as the band marches by. It means the ability to feel the pulse of a measure, a phrase, an entire song; to be able to sing full voice without speeding up or to whisper a line without loosing tempo; to innately know when to delay a note for effect, to compress or bend a beat within the overall pulse of the music. If you possess a sense of rhythm in this larger sense, put another check on the side of success, for you will sing with expression.

A *quick mind and a good memory*. Some of the brightest people around are singers. Frequently the music they learn, with tricky entrances and complex intervals, is as difficult as a mathematical equation. If a singer's career takes him or her to the stage, directions for acting and movement will be piled on top of the notes that must be learned. Add to that the possibility that the words to be sung may be in a foreign language. In today's fast-tempoed world of music, a singer is expected to be able to learn and memorize the music in a few days when he or she lands a job. "Minutes mean money," explains one TV producer. "There's no time to mess around."

A *good musical education*. The days when major singers were not expected to read music are gone forever. Today's professional singers are excellent musicians. Most working vocalists can sit down and play their own piano accompaniments. And it's not unusual for them to double quite capably on the violin, flute, guitar, French horn, or what-have-you. Unlike the old conservatory system, where the primary goal for singers was the production of a lovely tone, major universities, colleges, and conservatories now have high-powered music departments where singers are required to learn theory, music history, composition, and a variety of instruments. Most professional singers have college degrees. And, with few exceptions, all have been involved in music since childhood—piano lessons, school and church choirs, bands and orchestras. Pop singers are no exception, even though their music may sound deceptively casual and easy, for they number among the most knowledgeable and versatile musicians of all. It's the rare pop singer who walks on stage without an instrument in hand. Many write their own songs. Improvisations, intricate key changes, and complex harmony parts must come as easily as the sound of the singer's own voice.

Good health and physical stamina. Instrumentalists carry their music-making equipment in a case. They can take it out, blow on it, finger it, pull a bow across its surface, shine it up, and take it to a repair shop when it gets mechanically out of kilter. But as a singer, your instrument is you. It reflects your joys and sorrows, the amount of sleep you got the night before, the stuffiness of your nose when you have a cold. Like a dancer, a football player, or a circus acrobat, your career depends on the physical condition you are in. Singers who expect to sing for their supper for many years to come must respect their bodies and take care of them.

No matter what phase of the business you enter, singing takes a lot of energy. Many singers run, play tennis, or work out regularly to increase their stamina. If you are full of vim and vigor, you'll be able to count on a certain endurance level to carry you through a performance, rehearsal, audition, or any musical working day in top shape.

Tenacity. The singer on the way to success puts as much thought into the development of a career as does a physician, lawyer, or business executive. To outsiders, it may seem that many performers suddenly pop into fame as if struck by stardust on a magic night. But in fact, with very few exceptions, those performers have paid their dues, learned their craft, and made the rounds until the time was right to shine. They set career goals for the future, analyzed their progress, sang endless scales, picked themselves up from disappointment, and eagerly tried again with never a doubt that the songs they wanted to sing should and would be heard. Tenacity saw them through.

Do you have good, old-fashioned stick-to-itiveness? If so, your career will keep humming along through the inevitable ups and downs.

Talent. Did you think talent would head the list? Not so, unless by the word "talent" you mean the presence of large measures of the first six ingredients. While it's true that a voice of gorgeous proportions is a valuable asset in the classical music world, it's just as true that in the pop field that same sensational voice could never make the charts. A voice capable of splintering chandeliers at a hundred feet would certainly intimidate a classroom of children. Can you imagine a country and western singer tackling "The Toreador Song" from the opera *Carmen*? There are many fields in which an interesting quality, unusual expressiveness, innate musicality, or that elusive "something extra" are the talent tickets to a rewarding career. Let's call "talent" the ability to accept the sound that is you, to develop that sound to its fullest potential, and to find the niche that fits you best.

Those are the seven ingredients for success that will emerge as you read about the singers in this book. Because there is no other voice like yours, as there is no other person identical to you, your career as a singer will be distinctively your own. The path you follow to find success will not duplicate in precise detail any in this book. But the stories you will read will help to show you which doors to open, the basic skills required, areas where work is available, and, most importantly, the variety of ways in which you can sing for your supper.

First of all, let's enter Camelot . . . the make-believe but very real world of musical theater.

2

Musical Theater

Chorus lines, stage-door Johnnies, the understudy's lucky break when the star fractures a leg—everyone knows how musical theater goes!

And it's true that of all the music-making businesses, musical theater is thought by many to be the most romantic, the most fun, the most exciting and glamorous of all.

Every season, new Broadway shows go into rehearsal. Young singers answer audition calls and fill out cards asking for name, address, phone, voice, weight, height, coloring, age. They pencil in answers to the hard questions: Will you sing in the chorus? Are you a member of Actors Equity? What experience have you had? Then they wait nervously for their turn to show their stuff. Ignoring the knots in their stomachs, they smile confidently, sing sixteen bars, dance a few measures, and say a small prayer that the part will be theirs.

And when the part *is* theirs, rehearsal calls are posted for weeks of work to get the show polished and ready for the all-important opening night. With luck, the critics will write rave reviews and the run will be long. Songs from the show will be whistled and hummed from New Hampshire to Texas. Touring companies will take it out on the road. And if it is a well-loved hit—like *Oklahoma, South Pacific, Guys and Dolls, Carousel,* and dozens more—the musical will become standard repertoire for regional theaters all over the country for years to come.

The Music Circus in Sacramento, California, is one such regional theater that specializes in summer runs of long-time favorites. The fence surrounding the brightly striped canvas Music Circus tent is posted with fliers announcing the musicals to be performed before the season's end—*The King and I, The Unsinkable Molly Brown, Wonderful Town, Camelot, Irene,* and, opening tonight, the rock musical *Hair.*

How do you get to be one of the performers who sing and dance their way through these shows? Let's ask Judy Kaye, who is signed with the Music Circus for one week of rehearsal followed by a week of performance in the role of Sheila in *Hair.*

It is a hot afternoon in Sacramento, 102 degrees under the canvas tent, and *Hair* is in dress rehearsal. Judy, her shirt tied high over bare midriff and low-slung jeans, has just finished her big Act I number, "Easy to Be Hard."

"How do you get the jobs in musical theater?" Judy catches her breath and repeats the question. "By being versatile. That's the name of the game in this business. You have to be a triple-threat performer—actor, singer, dancer. And you better your chances if you've sharpened those three disciplines to a tee and are able to sing and dance in a variety of styles. The movements and vocal sounds of *Hair*, for instance, are a musical world away from *Carousel* or *My Fair Lady*."

In her mid-twenties, Judy has worked steadily as an actress-singer-dancer since her freshman year at the University of California at Los Angeles (UCLA) when she moonlighted after classes to play the part of Lucy in a two-year run of *You're a Good Man, Charlie Brown*. Now her résumé lists a long string of stage credits ranging from Kate in *Kiss Me, Kate* to Mary Magdalene in *Jesus Christ Superstar*.

Also spending two weeks under the Music Circus tent, playing the part of Woody in *Hair*, is Stuart Getz, twenty-two years old, small and wiry, with an unruly mass of curly red hair framing his freckled face.

Like most of the performers you will meet in this book, Stuart knew at an early age that he wanted to be a singer. "One of my earliest mermories," he says, "is of watching TV and wondering why that little kid got to do all those things instead of me."

But Stuart didn't sit and wonder long. Left on his own for a few minutes during a family vacation in Florida, he walked up to the hotel band leader, tapped him on the arm, and said he'd like to sing "When the Red Red Robin Comes Bob Bob Bobbin' Along." When he'd finished his show biz debut, a man and woman from the audience asked him which television performer he liked best. "At that time I loved Shari

Lewis and her puppets," Stuart says. Incredibly, the man and woman turned out to be Shari Lewis's mother and father. They put Stuart's parents in touch with a New York agent. "I didn't know what an agent was," Stuart says, "but instinctively I knew that something big had happened that would help me be that kid on the screen who got to do all those things."

And he was right. As a skinny first-grader, he put on his performing shoes and made TV commercials for a toy manufacturer. At nine, he played in the Broadway production of *Oliver*, followed by runs of *Ben Franklin in Paris* and *Mame*. "I started in the business as a six-year-old," he says, "and I've been at it ever since, learning as I worked."

College or on-the-job training? Stuart and Judy are examples of these two ways to prepare for a career. Which is best?

Paul G. Gleason is a good person to ask. Not only has he spent twenty years behind the footlights, but he is also the director of the Los Angeles-San Francisco Civic Light Opera Musical Theatre Workshop, a sort of finishing school in musical theater for people who are already professionals, or near-professionals. "You'll never land a role just because you have a college degree in theater arts," he says. "That alone is not salable. What is important is, are you trained? What can you do? You may have a diploma, but if the person behind you sings better, dances better, well . . ."

Many colleges and universities have active theater departments where students can learn a variety of skills under one roof. But it must be remembered that colleges and universities are in the business of turning out roundly educated people. Students with theater majors must still fulfill requirements in history, economics, English, and so on. It's impossible to work full time at perfecting "triple-threat" skills. Those who intend to make their living in the theater do as Judy did. At every opportunity—weekends, evenings, summers —they put their skills to work in campus and community productions.

"The very best possible course for pursuing a career in the musical theater," says Paul Gleason, "is to attend a recognized acting school such as the Yale School of Drama, the drama school at Carnegie-Mellon, the Juilliard School of Theater Arts, or the American Conservatory Theatre in San Francisco. At schools such as these you can work full time at learning your trade."

"If you don't go to school," Paul Gleason continues, "then you must search out the best singing, dancing, and acting teachers you can find and sign up for classes or individual lessons. You find good teachers by hanging around the business until you can ask the advice of people who are working in the legitimate theater. They know who the better teachers are." But he adds a hard truth: "It's not enough to have a 'knack' for the musical theater. You must know what you are doing. If you come on untrained, the professionals on stage will not tolerate your presence."

Both Judy and Stuart know what they are doing on stage. They are well-trained actors and dancers as well as singers. Judy's singing voice is full and rich, as capable of belting out a rock tune as a nostalgic love song, with a well-placed sound that could be classified as "legitimate pop." Stuart's voice perfectly matches his appearance—wiry and expressive. Both voices work equally well in musical theater.

Paul Gleason explains: "We hear a lot of 'hothouse' voices in auditions—a beautiful sound but no excitement. We pass them by." The voice that gets the part projects personality, characterization, and the meaning of the song. "Thousands of 'shower singers' have better voices than many of the people who earn their livings singing in the musical theater," Mr. Gleason goes on to say. "But the professional on stage is trained to achieve the effect of freshness, apparent lack of effort, and naturalness that is so pleasing to audiences. Trained, he or she can sustain that effect under any circumstance and maintain a healthy instrument."

Training—the sharpening of skills—doesn't end once auditions are won and a career is underway. For instance, when *Hair* closes in Sacramento, Judy will return to her home base in Los Angeles. She'll keep her "triple threats" ready for her next role with regular acting, dancing, and singing lessons. She'll stay healthy and trim with early-morning jogs around the park, daily calisthenics, and tennis matches with friends, all the while keeping a disciplined eye on the bathroom scales. "Performers can't get rusty and out of shape," she says. "Tomorrow I may be called for the biggest part of my life!"

Both Judy and Stuart spend a great deal of time making certain that they won't miss that part of a lifetime. Theatrical trade papers are regular reading—*Show Business*, *Variety*, and *Backstage* are filled with important information about who's who in the business, what shows are in the planning, what auditions are scheduled.

Once embarked on a career, it is important to be based where the action is—where auditions are held, where shows are cast, where producers and directors have offices. "Frequently I run into talented young performers who are living in places like Oshkosh, Wisconsin, or Eugene, Oregon," Paul Gleason says. "I say to them, 'Why are you living there?' Sometimes they may be working in community theaters where big-name professionals occasionally come to play special parts. But when those big names leave, if those young performers have any brains at all, they should follow them to places like New York, Los Angeles, San Francisco, Chicago, Seattle, where full-time legitimate theater goes on."

Stuart is on the phone talking with his agent. "Anything for me today?" He makes a note of an audition possibility and hangs up. With sixteen years as a working singer-actor behind him, Stuart knows the behind-the-scenes ropes of the business well. "If you show any promise at all, agents will find you," Stuart says. "But shop around. Take your time before signing."

Most fledglings in the business don't take the chance of being "found" and enhance their possibilities by making the rounds of agents', producers', and directors' offices to let their presence in the theatrical world be known. They carry their résumé of experience, a portfolio of professional photographs, and a "demo" tape (a recording of their voice singing songs in the styles in which they are proficient).

Stuart warns newcomers to keep in mind that big-name agents are often so busy working for their big-name clients that they may not put out much effort for a newly signed unknown. "It's crazy," he says. "Agents tend to put you on the shelf and wait around for you to become a star. Then they say, 'We handle a star!' and work hard for you." Lesser-known agents may try harder for a newcomer, but they don't get as many calls from casting directors. "Weigh the alternatives," Stuart says. "Try to find out what the agent's plans are for you before you sign on the dotted line."

Agents are paid 10 percent of the performer's salary. So why can't a performer find his own jobs, contact producers and casting directors personally, and pocket all the pay? Here's why: Casting directors prefer to work through agents. It's assumed that agents screen out untalented hopefuls and sign only legitimate professionals. It's also assumed that agents will send only those "right" for a part to an audition. Stuart says, "If you hear about an interview and contact the director personally, he'll say, 'Have your agent call me.'"

Stuart continues, "When you're new in the business, even with an agent, you still have to hustle for work. It's important that you not let your agent forget you. Agents have a way of saying, 'You're fantastic!' in the morning and 'Stuart who?' by afternoon. So you call them every day: 'Any interviews? Anything happening?' If they say, 'No, it's slow right now,' you feel awful. But the next day you have to be on the phone again. You begin to feel like a nuisance. Then—sometimes I think it's to keep you quiet—you're sent out on a call. If I hear about a call on my own, I'm on the phone again to my agent. 'Hey, I know about this interview. Why don't you send me up for it?' He arranges the audition, and if the part is mine, he gets his 10 percent."

What should hard-working agents do? They should steer their performers to the best teachers, help guide the direction of a career, talk up their client to producers and directors, set up interviews for suitable roles, bolster sagging egos when rejections come, and be on hand to applaud when things go well.

"Are you Equity?" rings in the ears of newcomers as frequently as "Do you have an agent?" Actors Equity is the professional union for performers in "book" shows, shows with a script. Equity members get first crack at auditioning for most parts.

"I can't work unless I have an Equity card, but I can't get an Equity card unless I'm working!" is the Catch-22 cry heard over and over from young hopefuls. But obviously the 16,000 members of Actors Equity joined somehow. How did they do it? By landing a part . . . somewhere. And one of the best "somewheres" is professional regional theater.

Let's talk to long-legged, auburn-haired Kerry Graves, who is signed to sing and dance her way through the entire Music Circus season in the ensemble. An important plus came with her summer-long job—Equity membership. This is Kerry's first year as a professional. "Up to now it was all education, lessons, and college productions," she says. Many producers of regional theater enjoy giving newcomers a hand up to the professional stage by signing them in apprenticeship programs, as chorus members, or in bit parts. Once a contract is in hand, union membership can be applied for. It costs several hundred dollars to join, a sum difficult for most young performers to raise. But many producers are willing to pay the fee and deduct it gradually from the summer's pay checks.

Kerry has made one other stab at professional theater—she has just returned from a six-month crack at the musical stage in New York. At summer's end she will return to the big time, but on this trip she will have her Equity card in hand.

Kerry describes the "open calls" (nonunion) chorus auditions she attended in New York: "Actually there's only a millimeter of hope because Equity interviews have already been held and all but a token bit of the casting completed. Nevertheless, hundreds show up. It's important to be seen. You take a number and wait your turn. It seems forever. Rehearsal halls, where most auditions are held, are huge rooms with dark green or brown paint peeling off the walls. Once we waited in a room under the stage and could hear singers and dancers thumping through their auditions overhead. But everyone is friendly. We're all in it together! The open calls gave me invaluable experience. But now when I go back, I can answer Equity calls and really have a chance."

Triple-threat skills sharpened to a tee, Equity cards and agents are all vital to a career. But one more thing is essential. It is what Paul Gleason calls will-you-work-in-the-business.

Every year the Musical Theatre Workshop headed

by Gleason auditions hundreds of talented performers —performers who can sing and dance, who can create a character, who are attractive to look at on stage. How is it possible to choose among them? "In some way, some give themselves away," Mr. Gleason says. "We know that they won't work in the business."

A positive response to the unspoken question "Will you work in the business?" means that a performer says yes to whatever is required and does his uncomplaining best: "Please sing the song a key higher." And the song is sung higher. "Louder, please. While hanging upside down."

The auditioner who impatiently asks, "I've been waiting forty-five minutes. When will I be heard?" may be heard, but probably not signed. He failed will-you-work-in-the-business.

Most newcomers begin in the ensemble, like Kerry at the Music Circus. Chorus members dress together in one crowded room, share precious mirror space, pass around tubes of makeup, and frequently share apartments during the run of the show. Performers who can adapt their egos and personalities to such close quarters will work in the business. In other words, they are troupers. There is no room in the theatrical world for the temperamental "star"—especially if that "star" has only begun to glitter.

Right now the actress's ultimate fantasy has come true for Judy Kaye. Not long ago she accepted the job of understudy to Madeline Kahn in the Broadway hit musical *On the Twentieth Century*. Three weeks into the show, the star developed vocal problems. Judy stepped into the role, completely prepared for "the biggest part of her life"—so far.

As far as Judy is concerned, there is no doubt—musical theater is the most romantic, the most fun, the most exciting area of all in the music-making business.

≡3≡

Musical Revue

All over the country, musical revue is coming into its own, offering opportunities for performers who can sing and dance with the best of them. Musical revue is part of the musical theater, but a revue has no scripted story line. A revue is a series of acts, gags, songs, and dances strung together in an order that may or may not follow a theme or make any sense. First cousin to vaudeville and old-time burlesque, musical revues are fast-paced, lighthearted entertainment striving for nothing more than uproarious laughter and delighted applause.

What does it take to be successful in musical revue? The same finely honed "triple-threat" skills that are so essential in the musical theater. But something extra is required—the ability to see the ridiculous in the ordinary and to react to zaniness as if something quite everyday were going on.

"Incongruity! That's what makes it funny." Saucer-eyed Nancy Bleiweiss, singing star of *Beach Blanket Babylon Goes Bananas*, finally settles on a word to best explain the success of San Francisco's long-running, zany musical revue.

"Yes, it's incongruity," Nancy says again. "The unexpected happens. A gorilla does a striptease. Christmas trees tap-dance. Glinda the Good, the good witch from *The Wizard of Oz*, sings rock 'n' roll. Our orchestra is four well-dressed poodles."

Beach Blanket Babylon Goes Bananas began by accident one summer evening on a San Francisco street —a happy accident that has resulted in four years of sold-out performances for the revue and has turned Nancy Bleiweiss into a professional singer-comedienne.

Nancy explains: "My sister Roberta and I, along with an old friend Steve Silver, were leaving a restaurant when we decided on a whim to sing along with a street musician. People threw money at us. We were astounded! So we decided to go home, put on costumes and see if we could make more. Steve is a costume nut—he has rooms full of them. Dressed in crazy things, we ran back to sing again. We really cleaned up!"

By midsummer, the motley entourage of costumed troubadors, which included an anonymous Christmas tree—"Steve has stage fright," explains Nancy, "and didn't want his face to show!"—a dead-pan Santa with a knee-length beard—"Roberta managed a bookstore and thought street singing didn't fit her image"—and a saucer-eyed Glinda the Good—"I bought tons of pink tissue paper and made ruffles everywhere!"—were a regular sight as they blitzed the streets with midnight musicals. They called themselves "Tommy Hail" after an itinerant roller skater whose suitcase Steve found in a junk store. "We knew his name because it was emblazoned in glitter inside the lid above his red high-topped skates," says Nancy. The trio carried the case as a portable bank in which passers-by could throw their money.

"It was much fun, so wild!" Nancy says. "If we didn't show up, people would miss us." It was there on the street that *Beach Blanket Babylon* developed. With no musical accompaniment other than castanets and a toy piano—"to get our pitch"—the trio improvised, tried and discarded ideas, and expanded their group.

Nancy is describing another essential ingredient—the ability to be spontaneous and creative. Since musical revues are not scripted, performers are constantly adding new bits of business. If the bits work, they become part of the show.

"Some nights," Nancy says, "there would be as many as ten of us: a 200-pound roller skater in pink tights, men in tuxedoes, a girl wearing a bathing suit and carrying a palm tree." No matter who came along to perform, Nancy was always there along with "Santa" and the "tree."

Then, like a scene from a 1930s movie-musical, Nancy, Roberta, and Steve asked each other, "Do you suppose if we hired a hall people would pay to come see us?" They did, and people came. *Beach Blanket*

Babylon opened for a limited run. "We brought in truckloads of sand and turned the theater into a beach," Nancy explains. "The audience sat on the sand —some even showed up in bathing suits. Our light booth was a lifeguard station. The guy who took tickets sprayed everyone's hand with Coppertone suntan lotion. If they wanted to go out and come in again, he'd smell their hands to make sure they'd paid."

Beach Blanket Babylon made enough money to put the cast and the orchestra on regular salary.

At the end of the run, *Beach Blanket Babylon* folded its beach umbrellas, shoveled up its sand, and moved to a permanent home in an old, ornate theater called the Club Fugazi. Tommy Hail's trunk was put away, and the revue took *Beach Blanket Babylon* as its official name. "For no reason," says Nancy. "We just liked all those Bs." *Beach Blanket Babylon Goes Bananas*, an all-new show, opened to critical acclaim at Club Fugazi and continues to pack them in.

Nancy is billed as the "star"; Roberta, director of publicity and public relations; Steve Silver, producer-director. But, in truth, all three pitch in to do whatever is necessary to make *Beach Blanket Babylon* a successful revue. Steve, in spite of stage fright, occasionally appears on stage as some heavily disguised object. Roberta shows up nightly as an M and M candy morsel, a tumbleweed in a country and western spoof, and, in her oversized suit and beard, as Santa.

"Featuring NANCY BLEIWEISS" reads the *Goes Bananas* program. And there is Nancy on the program's cover wearing one of the towering, fruit-bedecked headresses that have become her trademark.

"Steve has a creative mind that just won't stop," Nancy says. "At first, he made me a teeny little pineapple hat, about six inches high, to go with my Carmen Miranda costume. Everyone liked it, so he built it up to eight inches. The next night it was ten inches. 'I can't wear that, it's too huge!' I complained to him. But I *did* wear it, and the next night he made it even bigger. Now it's nearly as tall as I am and weighs I don't know how many pounds." Steve, flushed with the success of his towering pineapples, went on to top off Nancy's head for the revue's final madcap scene with a gigantic fruit skyscraper of enormous bananas.

Under the headdresses, Nancy, a natural-born comedienne, sings and cavorts her way through almost every scene in the show. She has that elusive "something extra," a certain comic flair—an essential for success in musical revue. A flair for the comic can be improved on, but it probably cannot be learned from scratch. People who have it are usually aware of their ability at a very early age. Nancy explains: "All my life, no matter how hard I tried to be serious, people thought I was being funny. At times it was painful for me. For instance, I had no confidence in myself as a singer. How could I? Even my teacher would collapse in laughter in the middle of my song. It was crushing. Now, I'm studying with someone who lets me be serious. I adore her. Yes, I'm a comedienne, but vocal rules apply whether you're singing "Three Blind Mice" or an aria from *Traviata*. My teacher has given me confidence in my voice and has helped me find direction in my life."

Nancy puts on her towering hats five nights a week

at Club Fugazi, with two performances scheduled on Fridays and Saturdays. She talks about the difficulty of accepting an understudy so that she might have an occasional performance night free. "One evening I felt ill when I arrived at the theater. As I put on my makeup I kept saying, 'I'll be fine. I'll be fine.' But when I put on my Glinda the Good wig, I knew I wasn't fine. I fainted just as the four poodles began my entrance music. On stage, they didn't know what to do. Someone tried to cover for me by singing my song, but they couldn't remember the words. Everything came to a halt. Steve made an announcement, we gave the audience refunds and, the worst part, they carried me out on a stretcher right through the middle of the house. Next day, we assigned understudies.

"It was hard to let someone else do a routine that I'd developed from infancy. I felt hurt. I can be replaced! But no one can really replace you—they can only take your place. My understudy did my lines, my songs, my characterizations and made them hers. She was very good. But she wasn't me. That realization helped me grow as a performer."

Nancy is well loved in San Francisco. At the opening of last spring's baseball season at Candlestick Park, she was invited to sing the national anthem. Who threw out the first ball? Frank Sinatra. At times, Nancy's real life resembles a scene from her own zany revue.

Right now, San Francisco's favorite singing comedienne has taken a big step toward stardom. She has signed a contract to appear on national TV. Saucer-eyed Nancy will hang up her fruit hats and try her wings away from the Club Fugazi.

"AUDITIONS for the newly revised *BEACH BLAN-KET BABYLON GOES BANANAS!* Open call for principal roles, male and female singers," reads an announcement in San Francisco's newspapers. "Prepare an up-tempo and a ballad. Bring résumé and music in own key. Performers without solid voice capability need not attend."

Opportunity knocks. Another singing comedienne will take Nancy's place. The show must go on.

4

Opera

What does it take to enter the world of opera, where a soprano trills a glorious farewell to life while dying of consumption? Where a bass sings full, round tones while accidentally stabbing his daughter who has hidden away in a burlap sack? Where bandits, swordsmen, mad kings, and lovers parted forever all go about their errands of romance and intrigue accompanied by arias, recitatives, and full orchestra?

What it takes is a combination of out-of-the-ordinary skills. First, a classically trained voice of unusual quality and generous proportion—there is no electronic amplification in opera to boost a voice to the topmost seats. Second, acting ability. Today's sophisticated audiences expect more than a beautiful voice. They expect a believable theatrical performance on stage. As one opera lover put it, "If I just wanted to hear a gorgeous sound, I'd go buy a record." In addition, opera is looking for people who are able to learn languages, cope with makeup problems, and deal effectively with other singers, directors, conductors, and the general public.

Right now, young opera singers who possess these skills have more opportunities than ever before. The Central Opera Service, under the auspices of New York's Metropolitan Opera, lists more than 250 opera companies and workshops in the United States. In recent years, many of the long-established large opera houses have expanded their regular seasons to include touring companies, "brown bag" lunchtime performances, and apprenticeship programs. This expansion has made grand opera more accessible to the public; it has also created opportunities for young singers to make a decent living while they transform their first-class talents into professional artistry.

In this chapter you will meet John Davies and Linda Roark. Both are concerned about moving toward operatic fame too fast. "The trick is to say no to the wrong roles and wait for the right ones," they explain, "to not be wildly ambitious and accept every part that comes along." While they accept parts suitable for their vocal maturity, both continue to study, to perfect their techniques and to learn new skills—a never-ending process for all singers.

Now, off to the opera house to meet John Davies, baritone.

As is his custom, John Davies has arrived early at

the theater to make friends with the house. Tonight he will sing the role of Doctor Bartolo in Rossini's comic opera *The Barber of Seville*. He goes "out front" and chooses a seat in the back row to observe the rake (incline) of the stage, the pitch (slope) of the orchestra seats, and the position of the balconies as he imagines himself on stage. "Heavy drapes on the walls, and the ceiling goes up for ever and ever," he says to himself. "Acoustics not so good." And then he reminds himself, "Don't push. It doesn't matter if that reassuring echo doesn't come back. They'll hear you."

He walks through the still-empty house into the preperformance hustle and bustle backstage. "On performance day, I wake up with a single thought, 'I'm singing tonight,'" he says. "For that day, nothing else matters. I do boring things to pass the time, like washing my car. I sing a bit—lightly, perhaps hum a little. I try not to think about the evening ahead—to keep the adrenalin down so as not to peak before it's time to go on. All day, I can't wait to get to the theater. Once here, it has a calming effect."

Now working with tubes of makeup, John begins to transform his boyish good looks into crotchety old Doctor Bartolo. "I like to do my own makeup," he says, "because this is where the performance begins. I start to feel like Bartolo; my mood turns grumpy as my face changes into the character's."

Costumed and made up, John goes on stage to practice a tricky entrance through double doors that must be closed behind him as he removes his hat and cape. "How to get around the hat and off with the cape without getting caught in the door," he says. "I've sung Bartolo probably thirty times in the past year, but never without practicing this maneuver before going on stage. It bothers me to death."

On-the-job-training is how John developed his acting skills. The Boston University of Fine and Applied Arts, from which he graduated, didn't emphasize stage movement or characterization in its opera workshops. "In my first professional roles, I felt insecure as an actor," he says. "Doctor Bartolo, for instance, took me forever to find. I'd come home from rehearsal depressed. Finally it was a question of letting myself go, of not worrying about being absurd. Only then did I begin to feel the physical Bartolo, and finally the emotional character." From that beginning, he studied everything he could about the art of acting. "I read about it in the afternoon and applied it at night."

Recently John sang an audition for a new teacher, who commented that she had seen him in performance. "I was hoping she'd say, 'You have a fine voice,'" he relates. "But instead she said, 'You're a fine actor!'" To the thespian trained on the job, it was a bigger compliment than he had hoped for.

"When opera is good theater, it's tremendously moving and exciting," he comments. "When it isn't, it's every bit as silly and bad as I thought it was at age fourteen when I used to make fun of it."

Now John finds a quiet spot backstage. It is twenty minutes until curtain time. He thinks through each entrance, reestablishing what he wants from each scene. "I consider, 'Where was Bartolo before he came through that door? What is his relationship to the others on stage?' "

He doesn't worry about how he will sound. "I've studied long enough, spent enough time and money, to know that my voice has a certain proficiency that I can depend on." And he no longer worries about on-stage memory lapses. "That used to be a big concern. In conservatory, I'd go over and over the music on performance day. I'd burn myself out. Experience has taught me that I won't forget. The only time I slip up is if I let the thought shoot through my mind, 'What if I forget the next line!' "

The stage crew makes a final check of the set as a wave of applause is heard through the curtain. Out front, the conductor raises his baton and the overture begins. Doctor Bartolo listens for his entrance cue, and in spite of heavy drapes and high ceiling, John Davies' rich baritone carries easily over the orchestra to the back seat of the house.

"After a performance I feel sensitive and vulnerable. I come off stage, and if someone says I did a good job, I don't believe him. If someone makes a minor suggestion, I take it personally. Twenty-four hours later, I would find the criticism constructive. So I try to talk only to my wife. We skip after-performance get-togethers and go home."

John's next goal is to speak five languages well. He has given himself eight years for the project. "If you want a topnotch career, you must be proficient in at least four," he says. "And it's not enough to be able to learn the words by rote and have a rough idea of the meaning." His aim is to learn each language thoroughly, to understand nuances and colloquialisms, in order to act and sing his roles with complete conviction.

"All of the big opera houses, in the United States as well as in Europe, are foreign-speaking," John explains. "Imagine a rehearsal if you don't speak the language. There you are—the conductor is Italian, the stage director is Italian, the cast speaks Italian— except for one or two of you who are nudging each other and saying, 'What'd he say? What'd he say?' You miss so much!" With five languages tucked tightly under his belt, John will feel at home wherever he sings.

Italian, German, and French are the big three languages in opera. John has mastered the pronunciation and has a general understanding of each. Italian, the most important language for classical singers because of its pure vowel sounds, will be the first he will tackle in depth. "I'm going to burrow into Berlitz for three months of intensive study. They promise I'll come out speaking like a native." Right now, he is also taking weekly lessons in Russian: "There's lots of Russian operatic literature and not too many performers who speak it well."

John realizes that any out-of-the-ordinary ability he possesses puts him more in demand and acts as an extra dividend to the upward progression of his career. "When a director knows you have a special skill, he keeps it in the back of his mind: 'How can I use that guy?' Knowledge of Russian, swordsmanship, dancing ability—I'd like to juggle. Now that's an area of expertise that would catch a director's eye!"

As we meet Linda Roark, soprano, she is talking about juggling, too. But she is not tossing clubs and balls in the air. Instead, she is juggling the demands of a career with her deep wishes for an ordinary private life.

All performers—both men and women, whether they sing classical or pop—must pick and choose to some extent from the kinds of alternatives that confront Linda, for active careers are almost synonymous with rootlessness.

There is not much about Linda Roark that fits the classic picture of a temperamental opera star—no breastplates and horns, no fifteen pieces of luggage piled imperiously behind her. Casually dressed in pants and bulky sweater, she could be the girl next door. In spite of successes that keep her traveling from opera house to opera house, here and abroad, she is still very much the girl from Tulsa, Oklahoma. In many ways, Linda Roark is a reluctant diva.

"I have this clothesline theory," she says. "In our backyard in Tulsa, there is a clothesline strung between two poles. One end is in the open sunshine, the other is hidden in the shadows of bushes and trees. The drift of my life, my career, is like the clothesline.

"I grew up ready to pattern my life on my mother's —a sunny, happy life with marriage and children, the bright end of the clothesline, familiar, easy to see. But at the other end is my career—shrouded, mysterious, the future unknown. For twenty-four years my life was influenced by the sunny side of the clothesline. Yet performing is my life's blood. I see myself drifting one way, then the other. I have an awful feeling that I will always be hanging in the middle."

Last year Linda married—"That emphasized the sunny side," she says—but to a fellow operatic artist— "back in the shade." She explains that their life together does not lend itself to roots. They are both continually on the move. "Our belongings are stored in Minneapolis, Chicago, San Francisco. It's a very hard thing to swallow that now I have no home. I can't get used to it. I don't like it."

At the same time, Linda is hooked on performing. She tells a story from her childhood. "We'd stopped at a café in Durango, Colorado. I was two. "On Top of Old Smokey" came on the juke box, and I sang the whole thing. Everyone in the place applauded. Pretty heady stuff for a two-year-old. My family will never let me live that one down!"

At three, Linda sang in her church youth choir. "The average age to begin was six, but the director thought that since I could carry a melody he'd let me sing." Later she studied piano and ballet. "I was totally inept at both, but I adored the rhythm and music."

In high school, Linda sang leading roles in school productions. "I was a lousy dancer, hopeless at the piano. The only thing left was to sing!" She began voice lessons in ninth grade. "I wouldn't advise anyone to start that young. But for me as a skinny, too-tall, awkward adolescent, it gave me an identity. I was 'the singer' in my high school."

Even so, Linda never thought her voice was special.

"I figured I'd teach for a while and then get married." At Tulsa University she earned her teaching certificate and studied with a teacher whose interest was choral music, not opera. Linda assesses the experience: "Pure luck. Just what I needed. I wasn't pushed forward or held back. My voice had a chance to develop richness and quality."

Linda bided her time. Instead of teaching, she went to work in a real estate office. In her spare time she studied with a new teacher, head of the university opera department. "He said, 'You should be singing opera.' I said, 'What a bore!'" He put the music in front of Linda, handed her roles. "I sang it. But I didn't particularly like it."

Then her arm was twisted again. She was talked into auditioning for the summer apprentice program at Wolf Trap Farm Park in Vienna, Virginia, a national park for the performing arts. The apprenticeship was hers. Linda pinpoints the experience as a turning point. "It was the first inkling that others liked my voice, not just the kind people in my home town."

Career opportunities skyrocketed in the life of the reluctant diva—a contract with the Dallas Civic Opera chorus, a second year at Wolf Trap, then a winning audition with Western Opera Theater (the touring arm of the San Francisco Opera made up of young singers). "My world did a flip-flop," Linda says. In between, she sandwiched in a master's degree in music from Southern Methodist in Dallas, Texas.

More awards! More auditions! More contracts! "Linda Roark wins $5,000 grant to help advance her career," announced the National Opera Institute.

"Linda Roark is first-place winner in District Metropolitan Opera Auditions," read the newspapers. Then followed a summer on scholarship at the American Institute of Musical Studies in Graz, Austria.

"When you're in the business, you hear about contests and awards—mostly by word of mouth," she says. "Someone asks, 'Are you doing the Western Opera Theater audition?' So you do, and hope you win instead of them! And you begin to be known. One right person you've worked with says to another right person, 'You should hear this chick!' And you get the contract."

Linda looks back over her operatic track record: "I know it seems impressive to someone on the outside looking in. But experiencing the reality of it day by day—it's simply the way I live my life."

Linda talks again about the clothesline in Tulsa. "I was given a talent, but I was also given a particular background to deal with. Am I supposed to be a wife and mother? Am I supposed to have a wildly successful career? Should I compromise and have a mediocre career? No career?" And then, "Can't I have both? Do I have to choose?"

Then her thoughts turn to a particular performance, a performance when everything was musically and vocally right. "I didn't feel particularly well or in good voice that night," she says. "But when I opened my mouth, it was all there, it all clicked. The audience came to its feet. There were bravos, curtain calls, bouquets of flowers." Linda Roark laughs. "It was almost as good as Durango, Colorado!"

5

Concert-Recital

The main difference between concert-recital singers and operatic singers is that concert singers stand more or less still while they perform. And while they sing, they appear as themselves, not as a character in a play. As in opera, the concert-recital stage takes a classically trained voice of great expressive quality and carrying power, a knowledge of languages, stage presence, and the ability to get along with other musicians.

While some singers sing for their supper only in concert, it is not unusual for classically trained singers to carry on dual careers, to fill their performance calendars with concert and recital tours interspersed with a few operatic appearances. Faye Robinson, lyric soprano, and Lenus Carlson, baritone, do just that.

Both singers are signed with Columbia Artist Management. Their appearances—whether in recital, as guest soloist with symphonic orchestras, in oratorio, or in opera—are all booked through the prestigious management service, whose offices are on New York's Fifty-seventh Street, directly across from famed Carnegie Hall.

For both singers, the leap to internationally famous concert stages was a big one. Lenus Carlson, blond and Nordic looking, spent the first eighteen years of his life in the rolling farmlands of North Dakota—"an area where an art song is seldom heard," he says. Yet, Lenus is quick to add that although the rural environment of his youth was not filled with what is normally thought of as cultural advantages, it was a good place for a fledging artist to grow aesthetically. "I lived next to nature in the wide outdoors. My development was free and natural, our home encouraging and loving." He talks of singers who grew up surrounded by art, symphonic music, the theater, and concerts with early exposure to languages. "I just had to work a bit harder to catch up," he says.

Faye Robinson had some catching up to do, too. With nary a thought to a singing career, Faye, a black girl, graduated with a B.A. in music education from Bennett College in North Carolina, with a major in organ. "I'd always sung in choruses," she says, "but never as a soloist." Faye began to teach school. Her brilliant soprano might never have surfaced from her classroom had she not decided to enroll for graduate work at Texas Southern University. "And, as usual, I signed up for the chorus," she says. A week into the semester, the choral director asked Faye to come to her studio for an audition. "I said that I had nothing to sing," Faye relates. "I knew no songs, no arias. All I knew were choral parts!"

But the choral parts were enough to verify the director's suspicion that Faye's voice was one of exceptional promise. "I began to study, but not very seriously," Faye says. "After all, I was a teacher and an organist, not a singer." Then Faye entered and won the Metropolitan Auditions for the Southwest region. "That gave me an inkling that I had a little something to go on."

More awards came her way. Faye decided to leave the South and try her wings in New York City. There she found herself surrounded by singers who'd been exposed to fine classical music for years. "And I'd just seen my first opera!" But by this time, Faye believed in her talent. She was ready to work at a singing career.

Faye found her voice late. Lenus found his early. As a boy he sang to the birds in the open fields, and he sang for his friends, his neighbors, his family. "I sang naturally, without any self-consciousness, for the pure joy of using my voice," he says. His unusual talent made him a standout in his rural community of Cleveland, North Dakota (population 100).

Then Lenus was off to Moorhead State College in Minnesota to earn his B.A. To help pay for his education, he sang at a local television station, a biweekly program. "I sang show tunes, old favorites, and lots and lots of hymns." He began voice lessons.

"At eighteen I sang freely and enthusiastically," Lenus says. "I had good coordination, a healthy body, and a desire to communicate the words of my songs. All were good values—key things, in fact, that made me a good singer. Then I began lessons. My teacher had traveled the world over; he'd heard fantastic singers. He set out to develop my voice—make it richer, more mature. He began to manipulate my sound.

"I believed in him because I was young and impressionable and he was intelligent, sophisticated, experienced, knowledgeable. I tried to do what he wanted. Now I know that it was absolutely wrong of him to impose on my young instrument his artistic and tonal values. He almost wrecked my voice.

"By some lucky instinct I stopped believing in him and left. But after only eight months with that guy, the joy, the enthusiasm, the freedom of communication with song—those key ingredients that made me a good singer—were ruined. It took me two and a half years, working with another teacher, to turn the corner and come back."

How can young singers know whether or not to put their trust, their future career, in a certain teacher's care? Two guidelines come from Lenus's experience. "First, if you can find a teacher who maintains your enthusiasm for singing, the simple joy of singing, you are making important progress," he says. "Second, if each time you go to your lesson, you experience the vocal sensations, the good feelings that you love and remember, you have to say, 'This is right.' Then you can jump across the border of trust, ready to grow with what that teacher can offer."

Faye talks about the importance of study, even for singers with a natural talent. "I've always sung well. A few flaws here and there, I'm told—nothing major. But natural instinct will take you only so far in this business. It has to be improved upon. You have to know what you're doing, develop a technique that twenty years from now you can count on. It's important to be able to say, 'Aha! When I make that sound, feel that sensation, it's because I do thus and so.' There will be times when you feel ill, emotionally upset, tired. But the show must go on! Good solid technique will see you through. A teacher can help you develop in this way."

With no experience, how can young singers find teachers that are right for them? It is important to listen to a teacher's students. Are they singing things well within their capabilities? Do they sound comfortable and sing without strain? "If they turn red, run fast," says Faye.

Find out what kind of career the teacher had. Although some fine teachers have not had a stage career, this is often an indication of ability.

"Ask singers whose voices you like who they study with," suggests Lenus. "And then find out for yourself whether or not you're on the same wave length, have rapport with that teacher."

While it's possible that even an inept teacher might be charming, rapport should be considered equally with other qualifications. "Your instrument is you!" Faye says. "If a teacher can't relate to you and what's in you, then it's a sign to look for someone else."

Because the voice is such a highly personal instrument, some teachers become overly involved with their pupil's lives and try to direct their personal attitudes and activities. As one experienced singer put it, "You're in the studio for a voice lesson, not a session on an amateur psychiatrist's couch. If they advise you not to smoke or breathe in cold air, or to get proper rest— fine. But if they persist in telling you who your friends should be or how you should deal with your family, you'd be better off in another studio."

Good teachers expect the most from their students. They pay attention to details, they are dynamic, they care about each student's development. And although they demand their pupils' best efforts, they begin with simple exercises and songs. "If you walk in as a beginner and the teacher hands you a big aria, forget it!" advises another professional singer.

And always remember that the first choice does not have to be final. "Audition" a teacher. Try him or her out. Work together and see what happens.

Lenus returns to "what might have been" if, in his college years, his instincts had not led him to a new teacher—"what might have beens" that pinpoint exactly the importance of thoughtfully searching for the right teacher. "After several years, I would have been singing badly. Singing badly, I would not have attracted public attention. Without public attention, I would not have had opportunities to sing. Without opportunities to sing, I would not have practiced. Without practice, my voice would not have improved. Without improvement, my enthusiasm would have dwindled. Lacking enthusiasm, I would have become interested in something else. I would not be a singer."

Instrumentalists find it a great advantage to get an early start on the skills and manual dexterity needed to master their violins, oboes, and pianos. For singers, this is not so. Boys should not begin serious study until their voices have changed and been given a chance to settle down. Girls, although they have no abrupt adolescent change of register, should wait until they are seventeen or eighteen. Most professional singers agree that there is no advantage in starting early and too many risks in doing so.

Self-awareness develops with maturity. And it takes self-awareness to be able to tell what is vocally right. Faye says, "It was no handicap that my vocal training started late. With no pushing or expectations of any particular sound, my voice matured in pace with my own maturity. I sang naturally, with no anxieties, no hang-ups."

But, unknowingly, Faye prepared herself in exactly the right way to be a singer. She became a competent musician. Her love of singing in choirs taught her to sight-read. Early piano lessons and later organ study prepared her to be an excellent musician. "Singers who know their way around the keyboard have a great advantage," Faye says.

One concert tenor, who neither sight-reads well nor plays piano, describes the slow, expensive process he goes through to learn his music. "I can't read notes from C to D," he says. "So I hire a coach to play my part over and over for me. He spoon-feeds me the music note by note. Sometimes I make a tape, take it home, and learn by rote. Either way it's time-consuming and costly."

"It's expensive enough to keep a career going," Faye adds, "lessons, clothing, travel, without having to pay someone to teach you the basics." Faye learns new scores on her own. Seated at the piano, she is able to see how her vocal line fits with the complete score. "Occasionally I see a coach—that's a person who plays the accompaniment and is knowledgeable about interpretation—if I'm not certain that I have the music securely under my belt. Sometimes when you sing and play at the same time, you're not quite sure you really have it down. If I'm in doubt, then I call a coach, get on my feet, and check it out away from the piano."

Right now, it's eight o'clock on a Thursday evening. Concert-goers are rapidly filling the auditorium in anticipation of hearing Lenus Carlson, baritone, in recital.

Tonight Lenus will sing his tenth performance of a twenty-city Community Concert tour. Traveling through the Midwest with him is his accompanist, Linda Jones, who is also his wife. It took Lenus three years to put together the combination of songs that he will present this evening. "I like my program, I never tire of it," he says. "And each audience is different. People give out an excitement that I want to give back. Each song that I sing reveals a bit about me. By the end of the evening the audience knows me quite well because of the shifting musical moods I project."

After the recital, Lenus and Linda will appear at a reception in their honor to shake hands, sip champagne, and accept congratulations. Then, back at their motel, Lenus will change from his elegant black dress suit into gray sweat shirt and pants for a midnight run. An outstanding athlete all his life, Lenus's starlit sprint in the fresh air will leave him relaxed, re-freshed, and ready for tomorrow's drive to another city, another auditorium, another concert audience.

In an eastern city, the final notes of the second movement of Beethoven's Ninth Symphony float backstage as Faye waits for the quartet's cue to come on. Unlike most conductors, who insist the quartet be on stage for all four movements of the symphony ("So we won't break the spell by traipsing on in the middle of things"), tonight's conductor has allowed the soloists to sit out the first portions of the work in which they are not involved. "It seems logical to me," Faye says. "This way we can hum and vocalize a bit backstage and come on all warmed up. It's awful to perch out there in front of everyone for close to an hour and then suddenly stand up and sing." The con-ductor lowers his baton as the movement ends, and Faye glides on stage with the others, her blue gown a subtle complement to the alto's soft lavender.

In talking about concert tours, Faye says, "Two gowns are the very least to take along. Zippers break, hems fall out, someone spills champagne on you at a reception. It's a good idea to pack a spare. Then, too, if you're singing in a quartet, you may clash with what the other female singer is wearing. One of the first things you ask each other at rehearsal is, 'What color is your gown?' "

Lenus Carlson has no such problem. When he's on tour, his usual costume is basic black—with or without tails.

At this point in her career, Faye finds that orchestral

and concert bookings come fairly easily. She would like to sing more operatic roles. She feels that there is a reluctance to cast her because she is black. "We've come a long way toward racial equality in this country," she says. "But I've reconciled myself to the fact that if I want a big career in opera, I'll have to go abroad. In Europe, I'm accepted for my work and not hampered by the color of my skin. So, for now, in the United States I'll sing those operatic roles offered to me and reconcile myself to the fact that the major portion of my career in this country will be in concert."

Faye Robinson's calendar is filling fast for the year ahead. Orchestral and recital appearances will keep her flying from one end of the country to the other. And along with the concert dates are a number of operatic performances. Faye mentally ticks through the bookings. "I'm not dissatisfied," she says. And then she adds with a knowing smile, "I just always want my career to go on a little better than it's going."

Lenus Carlson is looking over the flyers and press releases that his personal manager at Columbia Artists Management will send ahead of his appearances: "Ready for the big time." "He was magnificent." "Powerful, resonant and truly focused baritone." "High in the running as The American Baritone of the future," read excerpts from critical reviews. Lenus reflects, "If, when you begin, you have your sights set on being a star, you may be disappointed. Singers who reach a certain point and are unhappy because they are not big names have probably lost sight of why they wanted to sing in the first place—for the pure joy of it!

If a singer loves to sing and keeps working at it, he'll probably make a living. There are many places he can perform if he can be happy at his level." Lenus pauses to think over what he has just expressed. Then he leans back in his chair and fills the room with his baritone laugh. "But quite frankly, I don't think I'd be in the business if I didn't think I was going to be great!"

In the singing business, "greatness" can be measured in different ways. In the next three chapters, we will talk to singers who rarely, if ever, appear center stage. Yet they sing every day for their supper in careers that are exciting, fulfilling, and rewarding.

=6=

Music Therapy

Genola Spoonhour swings around in her chair, one finger marking her place in a book of African chants. Her blue eyes grow bright with anticipation as she talks about adapting the rhythmic chants to meet the needs of her patients.

Genola's office is in one corner of the bright and airy therapy room of the state hospital in Stockton, California. Her desk overflows with the tools of her trade —sheets of music, reference books, piles of records. Simple musical instruments—an autoharp to strum, a big tambourine, a glockenspiel, and Genola's ever-present guitar—crowd the nearby shelves.

But to Genola, the most important instrument she uses in her work is her voice. Genola is a singer who uses her musical talent to help other people find a happier, more satisfying life.

" 'A what?' That's the usual response when I say I'm

a music therapist," Genola says. "Or they politely say, 'That's nice. But I had no idea there were so many musicians in need of help!'

"Then I explain that a music therapist works with all kinds of mentally ill, physically handicapped, or troubled people and that music is the creative tool we use to help them experience greater self-understanding and function more successfully in the world."

It's no wonder that Genola finds few people knowledgeable about the work she does. Although the idea that in some mysterious way music can soothe the savage breast is as old as the hills, music therapy is a relatively new field.

Institutions first began to be aware of the therapeutic value of music after World War II. Emotionally and physically wounded veterans filled the nation's hospital wards. Volunteer musicians came to entertain them. But hospital staffs soon became aware that more was going on than momentary, happy responses to a song. They began to incorporate music into their rehabilitation programs.

By 1950, a handful of universities offered specialized courses in music therapy; one or two offered a degree. Today, twenty-eight colleges and universities across the United States have organized curriculums leading to degrees in music therapy.

"We're the odd-balls of the conservatory," Genola says cheerfully. "While the rest of the music students are into practice, practice, practice leading to perfection in performance, our main interest is in what makes people tick. Our schedules are loaded with classes in psychology, sociology, human behavior, anthropology, and group dynamics. But at the same time, we're expected to develop our talent. It's a terrific pull! At the conservatory I enjoyed performing, but what I really wanted was to get on with helping people."

The study of human psychology and hours spent in perfecting talent are only part of the music therapy curriculum. Also required are courses in harmony, conducting, composition, and ear training. Students learn to play woodwind, percussion, string and brass instruments. There are classes concerned with music in recreation, music in therapy, the psychology of music, and the influence of music on behavior. Finally, students intern for a six-month period in a community clinic under the guidance of a registered music therapist.

"It's not unusual for a student to enter the program and then wisely decide it's not for him," Genola says. "One singer dropped out when she came to the realization that she wanted the limelight, the applause. A performer, to do well, must be involved with self. A therapist must be more interested in the person with whom he or she works.

"A people-helping career has always interested me. I thought perhaps I'd be a social worker or a missionary. Yet music was a big part of my life. I took piano lessons, loved to dance, and performed at church and school events with my sisters. Somehow I felt it would all come in handy. And it has!"

Genola parks her compact car in the hospital parking lot and, arms piled high with "creative material," heads for her office. Her smile is open and warm as she greets co-workers and patients in the halls. A glance at her schedule tells her that a staff meeting will start her day.

"We meet frequently as an interdisciplinary team to discuss our patients' needs. My opinions are considered along with the staff psychiatrist, psychologist, registered nurse, and social worker on the case. We all see the person in a different way because our therapy tools are different. For instance, many things come to light in a creative experience that won't surface in, say, a talk session. Together we plan objectives and courses of therapy."

After the staff meeting, Genola returns to the therapy room to set up for a group session—ten young people hospitalized for drug abuse.

The room is large and sunny, with high ceilings. It's divided into informal activity areas. Today, one area is set up for an instrumental group—drums, piano, electric guitar, and string bass, along with a microphone. In another part of the room, comfortable chairs surround a round table. A phonograph and a collection of records is placed nearby. A bulletin board posts colorful record jackets and pictures of popular performers. Off this room is a small kitchen, where a group can have snacks or just meet in a homelike atmosphere.

One by one, the young people come into the room. Two carry guitars. Some respond to Genola's "Good morning"—others do not. A circle forms on the rug. Genola joins them, strumming her guitar. She begins to sing. The other guitars and a few voices join in.

A therapy session may take many forms. Today,

those who know guitar will teach others some chords to play.

"These kids are bright and articulate. But they've been hurt over and over again and have made crummy life choices. While we work together, I'm not interested in how well they play the guitar. Instead, I'm interested in how well they relate to each other and to me as a staff person, how they deal with their feelings, how they operate within the group structure. The group reinforces behavior. We can say, 'You did so well! What kind of feeling did that give you?' "

Sometimes Gena works with one person alone.

Judy had no family, no one she felt she could trust or turn to. At sixteen, she was silent, disappointed, and terribly hurt.

"When we began to work together, Judy didn't want to know me. But she did want my skills, of singing and playing the guitar. As I taught her, she began to open up. For Judy, singing was particularly threatening. It's such a personal thing! It's like saying, 'If you don't like my voice, you reject me.' But she learned to sing and express herself through the words of her songs while she played guitar. The experience was a significant gain."

Singing plays a major role in music therapy. While there are therapists who are trombone players, pianists, violinists—many kinds of musicians—to be successful they must be able to use their voices effectively.

"Therapists who aren't comfortable with their voices find the going rough. Things fall apart pretty fast if you can't lead out strongly, if you're unsure how high or low to start a song.

"My voice is the most fantastic therapy tool in my creative bag. Hum me a tune, and I know it. My ear is good. My voice is me, and I use it to bridge the gap between myself and others. Everyone has a voice—it's the instrument we have in common. Our voices tell a lot about us. As a therapist, my job is to help people become more spontaneous, more creative, less inhibited. My free voice leads the way."

Now Genola begins to work with a group of long-term psychiatric patients.

"Way down yonder in the brick yard." Her clear voice sets the jive beat.

"Remember me!" the group responds.

"Oh, swing your honey and turn around." Genola improvises a dance step. Singing and laughing, the group joins in.

"How do you measure the gain of participating in an exuberant dance routine? How do you measure a youngster free enough to sing a song? How do you evaluate eye contact with a man who hasn't met another's eye in twenty-five years? We must answer these questions every day," Genola says. "We are held accountable for everything we do. We must set goals for each case, decide upon the kind of therapy needed, and evaluate the results."

Genola is back at her desk. Patient progress reports must be filled out. Plans must be outlined for sessions to come.

"I'm loaded with ideas. Look at my shoe-box file!" Genola flips through the index cards crammed into the box. "This activity, this song, might be the one that will make meaningful contact."

Genola works in a psychiatric facility. But music therapists find their life work in many places. They are part of the therapeutic staff in hospitals, mental health centers, nursing care facilities, halfway houses, prisons, special education classrooms, camps, and clinics. They work with the deaf, blind, aged, cerebral palsied, mentally retarded, culturally deprived, emotionally disturbed, speech handicapped, gifted, or learning disabled.

"Wherever we go," Genola says, "music is our therapeutic tool. But we vary our creative methods to meet the special needs of those with whom we work."

Bright and alert, seven-year-old Robert talks like most children his age even though he has never heard another person speak. He discovered the ups and downs of speech by "feeling" music. With his hands pressed against the soundboard of a piano, he learned to interpret the vibrations he felt. A music therapist helped him as he learned.

Maria has muscular dystrophy. Her bamboo flute provides more than hours of enjoyment and a sense of accomplishment. The sustained blowing that it takes to play has slowed down the certain, eventual atrophy of her breathing mechanism. And now that she is old enough to know that she will not get well, her flute helps her express the depths of her feelings and emotions.

What makes music therapy work? Ancient people were convinced that music held mystical powers. Even today, therapists often find it difficult to explain why music frequently creates a response where other methods have failed.

In an effort to document the results in this relatively new area of therapy, the National Association of Music Therapists, the professional organization for people in this field, encourages those in the clinic to report in a scientific way their methods and findings. Research thus far leaves no doubt that music does cause an interaction between an individual and his environment, an interaction that often has "magical" results.

What do these "magic" music therapists have in common?

A concern for people. They believe that their job is to reach out and help others realize their fullest potential.

They are tolerant of all kinds of music. Although their own preference may run to Puccini arias, they open their minds to a foot-stomping country and western tune if that may hold the key to response. "We believe more in people than in notes, measures, and rests," Genola says. "Music is the tool I use, not an end in itself."

Therapists are innovative and creative. "There's no book of rules to tell you what to do when and where. We're always on the lookout for new ideas that may create beneficial responses. African chants, for instance, were not written with therapy in mind. But I think they'll reach my group. I'll try them."

Music therapists are pioneers. They may be the only ones in their facility or community, or even in their part of the state.

Take, for example, the case of Jimmy, a six-year-old autistic child. His mental illness locks him into a world where he views himself and others not as human beings but as objects. Jimmy doesn't talk. He spends hours rocking himself or swinging a piece of string. Jimmy's therapist has worked with many children, but never with an autistic child. Alone, she plans her strategy. First things first. She will try to get Jimmy's attention. She takes his small hands and claps them between her own, using a steady, rhythmic pattern. After several sessions, her first goal is accomplished. She has Jimmy's attention for a few short minutes of the time allotted for his therapy. Now she begins to sing rhythmically while she claps her own hands—"What's your name?"—and then his hands—"Jimmy." Her goal is a response. Finally, it comes. Jimmy claps by himself the two beats of his name—Jim-my. With each small step Jimmy takes toward normality, the therapist revises her goals. Jimmy's therapist is a pioneer.

Another quality therapists have in common is a deep belief in music's ability to effect changes in people.

"At the university, we were asked to think back on our own lives," Genola says, "to remember in what ways music has been helpful in our own development, in our own good feelings about ourselves. In order for us to use music to make important changes in others' lives, it must have made important impacts on our own."

Successful therapists must have a sense of humor and patience. "We work with people with very real problems," Genola explains. "But there's always a lighter side to life. We share with them our ability to laugh. And patience, because progress is slow, is measured in flickers of awareness, momentary response. We motivate, then patiently wait for those with whom we work to take their own steps."

Music therapists need to be competent and versatile musicians. Those at home in their work are skillful sight-readers, have good ears for music, and can harmonize and improvise easily. It's helpful to play piano or some sort of accompanying instrument, to be able to play spontaneously without having to find the music for a song in a book.

Every therapist's bridge to communication is his or her specialized talent. Genola's is her singing voice. "When I work with a group, I forget how I'm sounding. I don't think of myself as performing, although actually I am. Quite often a group is listening only to me. So I'm glad I sing well. The group says, 'Wow! She's really good!' They need and want to respect me. And yet my purpose is not to perfect a performance. What it comes down to is that singing is my significant ability, and I make the most of it."

Genola is at work in the clinic's therapy room. She sits cross-legged on the rug as she sings to her group:

> "In summer, winter, spring or fall,
>   What special thing tastes best of all?"

The words are direct and simple, the melody short and easy to remember.

The group of psychiatric patients listens to her warm, easy voice, and she encourages them to sing along. Then, in turn, each person tells what tastes best to him: "A snowflake melting on my tongue." "Cherries fresh-picked from the tree." After each response the song is repeated.

Genola is not interested in how beautifully the group sings. Nor is she looking for clever answers to the song's question. No one need be stumped.

Twenty-nine-year-old Ralph sits next to Genola. The group looks at him expectantly when his turn comes. He stares straight ahead. Genola waits and then, without comment, cheerfully moves on to the next in the circle.

For the first few sessions of Ralph's therapy, he strung words together into meaningless gibberish. Lately, he has lapsed into silence.

Now, Genola introduces another chantlike song:

> "Alike and different, alike and different,
> We are both alike and different."

"You have blond hair, I have brown, but we both wear shoes," one volunteers. The group nods approval.

"You are tall and I am tall, but I'm lots fatter than you." Everyone chuckles.

It's Ralph's turn. The song is sung, the group waits. Genola is about to move on. Then, without raising his eyes, Ralph quietly and hesitantly says, "I'm a man and you're a woman, but we both like to sing."

Genola looks at Ralph for a moment. Then her face breaks into a grin. "Wow!" she says softly. "Isn't that beautiful?"

Teachers

Teachers, like music therapists, enjoy a soft spotlight as they sing for their supper. While the brilliant lights of a stage career literally make it impossible for performers to even see those who come to listen, teachers share their love of music intimately with those who hear their voices—an experience that the three teachers you will meet now would not exchange for all the bright lights on Broadway.

Sue Metz stands before a class of third-graders. "Let's turn off the lights so we can feel soft and easy," she says. Recorded mood music plays in the background. Sue begins to move her arms and hands in time to the music. The class mirrors her movements. A chubby boy, wearing rumpled jeans and striped T-shirt, his face still flushed from recess, volunteers to come forward. Sue relinquishes her role as leader, and the children imitate their classmate's movements. "What we're doing here," Sue explains, "is improving rhythmic response."

In a center-city, all-black high school, Phil Reeder improvises an accompaniment on an electronic keyboard. It's spring vacation, but his forty-two-voice singing group, The Castleers, have come in for a special rehearsal. They leave Monday morning for a competition in Mexico City. They think they have a good chance of placing well with Phil Reeder's arrangement of Duke Ellington's "Satin Doll."

Walter Lamble is taking a lunch break at his desk in the crowded office he shares with another member of the university faculty. He's eating plain tuna fish today in an effort to skim off a few pounds from his portly figure. Between forkfuls, he answers the phone and talks to a fellow faculty member, chats with a student who knocks at his door, and confers with his office mate who has dropped in between classes.

Sue, Phil, and Walter are all young singers. They are also teachers. Sue is an elementary music supervisor. Phil is in charge of Castlemont High School's vocal program. And Walter is a teacher of future music teachers, a member of the music education staff at a large state university.

"If I were to list the qualities it takes to be a successful music teacher, energy and enthusiasm would head the list," Walter says.

Those musicians who are good at their teaching jobs believe that the subject they teach is not an optional frill but as much an educational basic as reading, writing, and arithmetic. Their obvious enthusiasm underlines the enjoyment, the life enrichment, the emotional satisfaction of expressing oneself through song. "It's important," Walter says, "for the future teachers I work with to know that I love what I'm doing. How awful if they thought I wasn't into my own field! The enthusiasm I bring to my work is passed on through them to their young students."

Sue agrees. "You always have to be up, ready to go. This is especially true for a teacher on the elementary school level because you see the kids only twenty or thirty minutes each week."

Like most music educators in the lower grades, Sue travels from classroom to classroom carrying her bag of musical tricks along with her. In some school districts, music supervisors are hired for one school. In others, they are expected to schedule their week between two or three. "I don't see the kids as frequently or for as long as I would like," Sue says. "But I aim high. My goal is that everyone in my classes will come out feeling that music is a good and happy thing, not some unusual form of punishment."

Phil, a bushy Afro topping off his mod-cut casual clothes, has strong feelings about the importance of music, too. "Music rounds out a person," he says. "It brings beauty and fuel for imaginative thought to kids in the ghetto. It enhances the life of youngsters who live in big houses on the right side of town. Music is a vital thing. It makes life worth living."

There's no doubt that Phil's love of music has directly enriched the lives of his students at Castlemont High. This morning their belongings make a mountain of suitcases at the air terminal. It's thirty minutes to boarding time; the Castleers are off to Mexico City. A few semesters ago they sang their way through Belgium, Holland, Germany, Switzerland, and France. "Some of the kids had never been out of the city before," Phil says.

The Castleers are proud of their group and proud of the music they sing. Their program runs from Haydn and Mozart to rock, gospel, and jazz. "When the kids first come into my classes, all they want to do is rock and gospel," Phil says. "For most of them, that's all they've heard. I try not to get upset about it. Little by little they learn to appreciate classical music, blues and jazz." Phil sits at the piano and improvises a rock accompaniment to a Mozart melody. "I may introduce Mozart to them like this, and they'll say, 'Hey, that's cool.' Then gradually I'll work in what Mozart had in mind."

What Phil is describing is musical patience, another quality good music teachers have in common. Sue sums up her philosophy about musical patience: "You never lower your standards, but you have to know where to begin. And then be patient with the rate of progress."

Outstanding musicianship is another essential. Sue, Phil, and Walter all know what they are talking about when they stand in front of their classes. They are excellent musicians who sang their first notes in church choirs—"I don't know if I had a good voice as a child," Walter says with a laugh, "but I know I had a loud one!"—practiced long hours on musical instruments, and made music a central part of their lives all through school. "When I graduated from high school,

I didn't make the commencement speech, I sang the solo," Sue recalls.

Walter and Phil entered college as piano majors, Phil with the goal of a concert career in mind. Walter speaks emphatically about the importance of a background in piano for all singers. "Whether you turn out to be a performer, a teacher, or whatever, the piano is where the mind is taught the physical concepts of high and low. You learn exactly how far it is between C and D. Intervals, pitch, rhythm, melody, and harmony structure—it's all right there on the keyboard. It's true that all of these things can be learned in ways other than piano, but the piano is the only place where you can learn them all at once." Sue bluntly adds, "I can't imagine a music educator who can't play the piano—and play it pretty well."

Right now, Sue's chorus, made up of fifth- and sixth-graders, are seated in choral formation in the school cafeteria. The hot-dish-of-the-day lingers in the air as the choir launches into a practice session on a medley of songs from the movie *Tom Sawyer*, which they intend to present at the annual spring concert. Sue directs from the piano as she plays the accompaniment. She signals a stop. "I want to hear all those T's and D's!" Sue's mezzo-soprano voice demonstrates the diction she wants to hear.

Teachers of vocal music use their singing voices all day long, but in the classroom their goal is to teach, not perform.

"My voice shows them what good singing is," Sue explains. "For instance, most kids listen to pop artists who seldom sing high. The things I sing demonstrate that the voice has range. In time they begin to raise their voices."

In the classroom, Sue rarely uses her full voice. "A big sound can be intimidating and overpowering," she says. "The kids begin to lean on you. You stop, they stop. Or they listen to you and forget to sing. Or they get giggly because a full-powered, trained voice sounds artificial and stagy to their ears. Sometimes I catch myself singing along, having the best time, and then suddenly realize that I'm performing and the students aren't participating. I try to keep it down. But sometimes in chorus, I indulge myself and let it fly!"

It's not that Sue, Phil, and Walter are short on performing skills. The smell of grease paint and the heady sound of applause are as familiar to them as the squeak of chalk on a blackboard. Between them they have performed in enough college productions, soloed with enough symphony orchestras, participated in enough choirs, taken bows in enough community theaters, and entertained in enough night clubs to satisfy the performance needs of a dozen singers. All three enjoy their communities' applause as church musicians and as soloists in a variety of musical events. "When did I know that I wanted to teach rather than go into the performing business?" It takes Walter a split second to answer his own question. "It was the first day I walked into a classroom and started teaching. For me, performing is never as fulfilling."

Phil continues: "My mother was a professional singer. She sang in the French Quarter in New Orleans. Listening to her, I learned how to use my voice. I worked my way through school as a church musician and as an entertainer in night clubs. So it's not that I'm short on ego—I have plenty of that. But I'd rather hear my choir applauded than me. In fact, when my kids are well received, that *is* me!"

As Phil sees it, part of his job is encouraging the performance hopes of his high school students. "My kids have dreams. They see themselves becoming another Gladys Knight or Stevie Wonder. What's wrong with dreaming?"

There are many places where high school and college students can turn performance dreams to reality as paid nonprofessionals. According to Walter, who spent his college summers working in shows, "There's a whole world of musical theater that is nonunion and not on the star system. They hire a lot of talent and often pay quite well."

Walter suggests that young performers who want to spotlight their summer employment write for a listing of stock theaters from their state Chamber of Commerce.

In addition to community theaters, Walter steers his performance-minded students toward dinner theaters and restaurants that feature singing waiters. "Quite often, too, resort areas and national parks hire summer entertainment," Walter adds. "If two or three kids put together a good, easy-listening group, chances are they'll be hired."

Theme parks, like Disneyland and Six Flags over America, offer outstanding opportunities to develop and polish talent. For instance, Opryland in Nashville hires over three hundred young singers, dancers, and musicians for their eleven fully staged productions. Auditions are held on twenty-one college campuses as well as in Nashville. "I advise my students to write directly to the theme parks to ask for audition information," Walter says. "And I also remind them that most places book their summer entertainment in January and February. If they start thinking about it in March, they'll probably be too late." And then he adds, "It's of prime importance for teachers in high school and college to keep up on performing opportunities and encourage their students to try for them."

Energy, enthusiasm, patience, outstanding musicianship, an ability and a desire to encourage their students' hopes and dreams—what other qualities do successful music educators have in common? Sue, Phil, and Walter answer unanimously, "The ability to work well with other members of the faculty."

It's recess time, and Sue, arms laden with guitar, records, and Latin American rhythm instruments, is on her way to a fourth-grade class. "Hi, Mrs. Metz!" "Can I help you carry something, Mrs. Metz?" "Are you coming to our class today, Mrs. Metz?" Children dance around Sue like frisky mice responding to the Pied Piper's call.

"Hi, Tim!" "No, I think I can manage it all, Lisa." "I'm on my way to your class right now, Danny." While Sue is a permanent member of the school's faculty, at the same time she is always a visitor, an exciting treat for a class, a welcome break in the daily routine.

"Because I am a visitor, the success of my program

depends on the support of the classroom teachers. They are the ones who prepare the children for my time with them. They release kids from arithmetic or whatever to come to chorus rehearsal. They keep music going in the classroom during the rest of the week." In turn, Sue makes herself available as a resource person for the teachers: "A unit on Japan? Yes, I have some great songs. And how about a recording of Japanese music?"

At Castlemont High School, Phil's Castleers would find it impossible to take off for Mexico or Europe without the cooperation of Castlemont's teaching staff and administration. Phil explains, "At Castlemont we've established the School for the Performing Arts. The school offers individualized and small-group learning with flexible scheduling so that our singers can maintain their scholastic standing while participating in the Castleers' heavy performing schedule. We all work together to make the school work."

What educational background does it take to become a teacher? "In many states, a master's degree is now considered a standard requirement for public school jobs," Walter says. "And if you'd like to teach on the college level, you should plan on getting your doctorate."

Both Sue and Phil have master's degrees in music education with an emphasis on voice and choral conducting. Walter is well on his way to completing requirements for a doctorate in music education and choral conducting.

How do you choose a school that will prepare you to

be a topnotch teacher? College catalogs, which can be requested by mail, often give a picture of the school's emphasis. Some are quite clearly in the business of turning out performers. Others, from their course listings, obviously value highly the training of music teachers. The music educator's professional organization, Music Educators National Conference (MENC), may be of further assistance.

Once a choice of college has been made, what about the curriculum? There are classes in music theory, composition, harmony, conducting. Singers are expected to enlarge their knowledge of the musical world by learning to play one instrument from each group of orchestral instruments—strings, brass, woodwinds. Weekly voice lessons are on-going through the entire four years. "When you teach," explains Walter, "it's not enough to understand how your own voice works. You must also know how other voices work." In addition, students are expected to sing in choirs and ensembles. An important part of the curriculum are classes that deal with the nitty-gritty of teaching—how to set up a classroom and make lesson plans. There are also hours of psychology that prepare the future teacher to deal effectively with people. "It's not easy to organize and teach a class," Sue says. "You've got to be prepared." Practice teaching, for a specified number of hours in a real school under the supervision of an experienced teacher, is one of the final requirements before accreditation.

"Every semester I have the responsibility of putting my name on pieces of paper that give people permission to teach," Walter says. "Signing these credentials is an awesome responsibility. I'm entrusting young minds to these new teachers."

How is the job market for young music educators?

"That depends on where you want to live," Walter answers. Some parts of the country are cutting back on specialists of all kinds because of lack of funding in their school districts. Other areas are experiencing lower enrollments, the result of a declining birth rate. "Wherever there's a student crunch or a money crunch, the so-called 'frills' are the first to go," Walter explains. "When school districts are on a back-to-basics kick, the first things they cut are those that make life worth living!"

Traditionally, the Midwest is strongly oriented toward public school music. Walter's experience is typical: "My first teaching job was in a Midwest high school with a total enrollment of 800 students. Yet I was one of three vocal teachers. Everyone sang in one choir or another."

In many school districts, music teachers teach a half-day of music and a half-day of English, history, math or whatever subject area they are accredited to teach. "It's safest for students to carry a double major," says Walter, "because right now it may be unwise for them to think that they will land a job that will allow them to teach only music." But then he adds, "Good teachers are always in demand. There is always a shortage of good teachers."

Phil's Castleers are back, triumphant, from Mexico City with a silver medal in the classical division for Haydn's "Kyrie Eleison" and with the big prize, a gold medal in the swing division, for their renditions of "What I Did for Love," "Mood Indigo," and "Satin Doll." But today there is music to be learned, polishing to be done for the Castleers' next performance.

Phil Reeder hits a chord on the piano. Forty-two voices respond. Phil Reeder smiles.

Church Musicians

Singers who sing for their supper as church musicians are part teachers, part performers, part spiritual leaders. They approach their work as a special calling, for in churches large and small, of almost every denomination, music has long been an essential part of congregational worship.

Right now, at the First United Methodist Church in Colorado Springs, 150 teen-age voices are raising the roof. It's late Sunday afternoon, regular rehearsal time for the Youth Singers, and they are working their way through a rousing spiritual.

"I shall, I shall, I shall not be moved.
Like the rock of ages, I shall not be moved."

With a hand clap, Charles Hausmann, First United Methodist Church's minister of music, signals a stop.

"Like this," he says, demonstrating a tricky bit of syncopation for the basses. "Got it? Everyone now. One, two, ready we go." Lilting voices and bright faces reflect their director's enthusiasm.

Charles Hausmann looks scarcely older than the high schoolers in his choir. "When I applied for the position here at Colorado Springs, I really wasn't supposed to be in the running," he says. "I didn't have the years of experience behind me that the screening committee felt was necessary."

Colorado Springs First United Methodist Church lists a 6,000-member congregation. The church is housed in an imposing structure that fills the better part of a good-sized block. The main sanctuary seats 1,800 parishioners. For more intimate services, rows of pews in the chapel seat 100. In addition, there is a 400-seat, fully equipped theater for stage productions.

A sixty-eight-rank pipe organ fills the main sanctuary with music on Sunday mornings. Both the chapel and the theater are furnished with smaller organs. "And scattered here and there throughout the church are forty pianos," says Charles, completing the keyboard inventory.

The performing choirs at First United include four major choirs of young children, the 150-voice Youth Singers, and a 145-voice adult Chancel Choir. Five handbell choirs rehearse and perform regularly. Three instrumental ensembles practice twice a month. Recorder players meet every Wednesday evening. The Sacred Dance Ensemble performs on special occasions. Two hundred children meet every Tuesday afternoon for a "Discovery" program of music, art, and drama.

Private or group instruction is available in voice, piano, and organ.

In summer, the church holds six worship services each Sunday, in winter four.

Charles oversees the entire program with the aid of an eight-number music staff. "Some are paid, others are volunteers," he explains. An additional volunteer staff of thirty helps as teachers, coordinators, and assistants. "My job is described as a full-time position," Charles says. "But actually it's all the time!"

Charles's music program in Colorado Springs is one of the largest of its kind. "When I was accepted here as music minister, I felt deeply honored," he says. "But at the same time, I felt a strong calling from God."

Charles has been serving God with song and music for most of his life. "My high school owned one of the biggest pipe organs in New Jersey," he says. "And I became the school's principal organist. Keyboards come easy to me."

In the ninth grade Charles took his first church job in a small church of fifty members. From there, still in high school, he moved to his home church to direct the youth choir and to shoulder the musical responsibility for one service each Sunday.

Many colleges and universities with strong music departments offer courses designed to train church musicians. Charles applied for admission to Westminster Choir College, a small school in Princeton, New Jersey, whose major emphasis is on church music.

"I entered as an organ major," Charles says, "an organ major with a strong desire to sing." From his voice teachers, he learned more than vocal technique, musicianship, and interpretation. They also emphasized singing as a means of total communication—a way of involving the entire body, mind, and spirit as an offering of praise to God and as an inspiration to others. "This philosophy penetrated deep, deep, deep into my soul," Charles says, "It unlocked the door to my voice. I found I was able to do things with my voice I had never thought possible—produce tones I didn't know were there."

A dual emphasis on keyboard, preferably organ, and voice is a happy combination for job-hunting church musicians. Many churches with limited budgets frequently hire one person who is expected to be the musical jack-of-all-trades for the congregation—a person to play for the worship services, conduct the choirs, perform as a soloist, and direct the musical life of the parishioners—all with equal proficiency. But even in larger churches that are able to hire specific people to be either choir masters or organists, the ability to move easily from one to the other makes for greater versatility within the program.

Charles's dual talents have always assured him work. Through his school years he moonlighted in his chosen career. From church to church he moved, each time to a position of greater musical responsibility, putting into practice the theoretical training he learned in his classes. At the same time he flirted with the idea of a secular vocal career, perhaps in opera, the concert stage, or the musical theater. He loved to sing.

Then twenty-three years old, Charles, who by that time had accumulated more than ten years' experience as a church musician along with a master's degree, was invited to join the faculty and administrative staff at Westminster College. "There I had the opportunity to share with the students my experiences, my knowledge. It was my destiny, at this time of my life, to train others to go out in the field."

As Charles entered his third year of teaching, he began to feel that Westminster Choir College was a protected environment. "It was time for me to return to the active music ministry. God has given me certain gifts—musicianship, a voice, the ability to be an effective leader. I felt it was again my calling to be a church musician."

Charles searched the country for a position where he could best make use of his experience and talents— "a position where I could grow musically, nurture many people, and develop a diversified program using instruments, voices, choruses. A church where I could do musicals, opera, and oratorios and provide the most effective music possible for the worship of a congregation." First United Methodist in Colorado Springs was such a church.

Few churches across the country have as large and varied a music ministry as does Charles's. However, although their work may be on a smaller scale, every church musician's work is similar to Charles's in Colorado Springs.

Church musicians are ministers. "Above all, I think of myself as a minister who ministers in a special way to the congregational needs of my church," says Charles. Church musicians believe that music is as effective a tool for worship as is the spoken word of the pastor. "Many people find it difficult to talk about their relationship with God," Charles explains. "Through music, especially the scripture verses that have been interpreted by composers, they can proclaim their faith, raise their voices, be inspired and inspire others."

The church musician's ministry is based on the belief that people become better when they raise their voices in song. Charles explains: "When we sing, we lift ourselves out of the realm of ordinary existence onto a closer plane with God. When body, mind, and spirit are involved with singing—which is exactly the way it should be—we offer our praises and our entire being to God."

When church choirs meet for rehearsal, their purpose is more than to learn the notes, stop and start together, and practice the song until it's perfected enough for the Sunday service. "We gather because it's important to use our voices, our gift from God, correctly. And as we sing in the best way we know how, we become refreshed and inspired. Singing renews the spirit!"

Charles believes that his ministry should extend past the walls of his church. "Churches should be community cultural centers as well as spiritual centers. Art, music, dance—secular as well as sacred works— are all appropriate in the life of the church. Right now, we're in the midst of a fully staged production of *The Music Man*, a musical show that the entire community will enjoy."

Church musicians are teachers. Charles's schedule includes time for private voice instruction. Today, a soprano from the adult choir has come by for special help with the solo passage she will sing in next Sunday's anthem. "It's exciting to help unlock the door to another person's voice, to watch self-assurance develop and the ability to communicate increase. Actually I like to think of myself, instead of as a teacher, as an 'enabler.' I teach others to enable them to teach others, so that they can enable others. That's the way God's work gets done!"

Church musicians are also administrators. In churches large and small, effective music ministers coordinate their programs with the other ministries of the church—education, youth, evangelism, social outreach, the preaching ministry.

It is Monday morning, and Charles is meeting with the pastor of his church to review yesterday's Sunday services: "How might we make the order of worship move more smoothly?" "Did the anthem enhance the message of the sermon?" Together they search for ways to improve the effectiveness of the work they do.

Later in the day, Charles will meet with his staff to delegate areas of responsibility. "We work from a calendar penciled in a year in advance," he says. "Music must be selected and ordered for each choir, each service, each special event." In addition, with the assistance of staff and volunteers, concerts and tours are arranged, choir seating charts made, absent members contacted. On Tuesday afternoons, Charles becomes the "principal" for the children's Discovery program and makes himself available as a resource person for the teachers of the classes. "And on and on it goes," he says. "If a church musician is not a well-organized administrator, he will never make music. He'll be caught up in meetings and paperwork."

Music ministers are skilled and versatile musicians. Charles's large church serves a congregation of varied backgrounds. "The theological stance of our membership varies from formal high church to hell-fire and brimstone," he says. "It's challenging to minister musically to this kind of congregation." Music is coordinated with the style of each service. Gospel hymns, standard church anthems, great oratorios, contemporary electronic music, folk songs, and rock are all equally considered. Charles sums it up: "All good music praises God."

In churches smaller than Charles's church in Colorado Springs, choir directors often are expected to conduct their singing groups while doubling as organists—a task that calls for coordination as well as musical expertise.

"But no matter what your duties or the size of your congregation, you must never let your skill as a singer sag," Charles emphasizes. "My singing voice is essential to my work and a source of inspiration to others. I would not be a church musician had I not been a singer first."

Charles quotes a favorite poem:

"How many of us ever stop to think of music
  As a wondrous magic link with God,
  Taking sometimes the place of prayer,

When words have failed us 'neath the weight of care.
Music, that knows no country, race, or creed,
But gives to each according to his need."

For Charles Hausmann and many other church musicians, their work is more than a full-time job, more than an all-the-time-job. It is a special calling, a way of life requiring dedication.

9

Gospel

It is eight o'clock on a Sunday evening, and Verlin Sandles is "in charge" at the Macedonia Baptist Church. Her clear, full-throated soprano meanders expressively through the jumped octaves and stretched blue notes—what the church calls "curlicues and flowers and frills"—of the songs that express her faith. Verlin Sandles is a gospel singer. She, too, uses her voice in praise of God, but she is a traveling troubadour who carries her messages of personal faith to audiences both inside and outside an organized church.

She sings of everyday trials and tribulations here on earth and of a better day to come: "This world is not my home. I'm only a stranger here. My home is up in Glory . . ."

The congregation of the Macedonia Baptist Church responds with a fervent "Amen." The collection basket is passed with a request from the minister, "We're not going to ask you for change. We're going to ask you for some green. Can't do much with change." Verlin accepts an armload of roses, and it's announced that autographed copies of her album, *I'll Be Happy in the Midst of the Lord*, will be on sale.

Verlin says, "People ask me, 'Why do you sing gospel music?' I say, 'Why not?' It's beautiful music. And the words—there's truth in them, even for people who are not religious. Gospel songs are about everyday troubles, worries, unhappiness—getting the food on the table. And the songs reassure that no matter how high, how low, how wide a problem, me and the Lord can battle it through."

In the black struggle for survival, song has long expressed the joy and sorrow, the love and hate, the hope and despair of black humanity. Whether in storefront churches or ornate cathedrals, songs invited the Holy Spirit to break into their lives "buildin' them up where they were run down and proppin' them up on every leanin' side." Though there be a hard row to hoe, a rough road to travel, they intended to make it through the storm.

Outside the church, black people sang the bittersweet blues of the "burden of freedom"—no money, no job, loving and losing, the isolation of being left alone. Blues are the gospel songs of the street. And gospel is pure blues with religious lyrics. Both have the same note-bending, the same "curlicues and flowers and frills," the same groans and moans and shouting, the same irresistible syncopation and swing.

In fact, gospel music has influenced every area of

popular music. It put the swing in 40's swing, the honest emotion in country and western, the beat and group vibrations in rock 'n' roll. The 1930 gospel tunes of songwriter Thomas A. Dorsey live again in the performances of Aretha Franklin and the Rolling Stones. As Marion Williams, a singer who has traveled the gospel circuit for thirty years, says, "Anything I hear—jazz, soul, rock—they got some gospel shouting snuck up in them somewhere."

Like most gospel singers, Verlin found her voice in church. "I've been singing since I was five. There was lots of music in our church—even an orchestra. My mother played saxophone, my father played piano and sang. My brothers didn't sing, but they had favorite numbers they liked to hear. At night, getting ready for bed, they'd say, 'Verlin, sing such-and-such.' And I would. Such fun!"

Old-time singers say they "came up on mother wit, and Jesus." Today's young gospel "shouters" are frequently college-educated musicians—high school is taken for granted. They are "young, hip, and saved," in the words of one older gospel singer.

Verlin is no exception. "I went to college, and there, for the first time, I had private singing lessons. How I enjoyed the formal training and the opportunity to sing classical music—opera, art songs in German, French, and Italian. There's no difference in vocal technique between singing gospel and classical songs." But while Verlin studied the classics, she found inspiration for the kind of music she loved most by listening to fine gospel artists like Mahalia Jackson, Sarah Jordan Powell, and James Cleveland.

Verlin still studies. "Lots of gospel singers sing hard —they push their voices to hoarseness. You can't do that if you want to keep singing. My voice is a gift, a natural thing. I just sing. Just sing!" But no matter how natural a voice, Verlin believes it should be trained. "Bad singing habits come fast and are a long time going. For instance, when I first went to the teacher I study with now, he asked, 'Do you have children?' And I answered, 'Yes, two little girls.' He said, 'You yell a lot, don't you?' I admitted that I did. 'You'll have to yell differently,' he said. 'You're smashing your vocal chords together. Breathe deeply, relax your throat, open your mouth wide . . .' Now, when I'm exasperated, I prepare myself properly to do my yell." Verlin pauses and laughs. "Usually by the time I've done all that, I've cooled down and say, 'Why bother?' "

It takes a phenomenal voice of great versatility to sing gospel. Most opera singers would think twice before tackling the skipped octaves, the intricate twists and turns that add emotion to the words, the whispered or sometimes shouted high notes that seem to reach to heaven on the musical scale. Added to that, it is unlikely that a gospel singer will ever sing a song the same way twice. Original, spontaneous expression is what gospel singing is all about.

Phenomenal voice or not, few gospel singers get rich. Verlin says simply, "My music is not entirely money-oriented." Marion Williams, known as one of the greatest jazz improvisationists in gospel, put it in the flowery language of gospeldom, "I've been way out on the stormy, raging sea, and God delivered me every time. That's just your lot if you're singing the gospel.

Your way's never going to be too easy. But do you know . . . I'd go through it all over again and thank him for my journey."

Most feel rewarded if they are able to make a comfortable living. Yet a few gospel stars, like James Cleveland, are able to set fees as high as $5,000 for a program. Others have grown wealthy from record sales. But such instances are rare. The gospel highway may be the toughest and most dangerous route to show business. Gospel crowds are small compared to the crowds that jam stadiums for pop events. Fans, though loyal, either expect the Holy Spirit to provide for their artists or have less in their pockets to shell out for tickets.

The work can be exhausting. The average big-name group travels on the road eight or nine months out of the year. Monetarily, small acts do best; fewer musicians have a stake in the pot.

"I've not reached the point where I earn my entire living singing," Verlin says. "But I'm confident that will be. My husband believes in me, encourages and pushes me."

In the meantime, Verlin is in demand for special programs and concerts. Every Sunday she sings either at her home church or as guest soloist in another. Funerals—"If they want to make a donation, that's fine. But I never set a fee for a funeral"—and weddings bring a steady stream of bookings.

Until recently, Verlin was known only in church gospel circles. Then she joined the cast of *Evolution of the Blues*, a long-running, theatrical musical history of black Americans' contribution to the world's music.

Newspaper critics wrote rave reviews: "One of the most poised and beautiful singers I have ever heard," read one.

"When I was approached to sing in *Evolution of the Blues*," Verlin says, "my husband and I took the music to our pastor, because we are Christian people." The Reverend gave Verlin his blessing.

The line that opens the show in *Evolution of the Blues* is, "Everything started in the house of the Lord." That includes pop music—jazz, rhythm and blues, rock 'n' roll, country and western—which evolved out of the rhythms and sounds of gospel songs.

Gospel expert Tony Heilbut wrote in his book *The Gospel Sound*, "If you're saved and a singer, your options are pretty well defined. You can stay in the church, guaranteed an appreciative if impoverished audience, or you can spread the word to audiences who couldn't care less about Jesus. In other words, you're either a consecrated singer or an entertainer." First and foremost, Verlin Sandles is a consecrated singer.

=10=

Studio Singer

Melissa Mackay, headset clasped over her long honey-blond hair, is perched on a stool in a motion picture sound studio. Alone in the huge room, she sings along while she intently watches a movie cut. She carefully times the words of her song to the lip movements of the actress on the screen. Her goal is to synchronize so perfectly that no one will guess the voice heard is not that of the woman acting the role.

Finally, when both Melissa and the sound technicians are satisfied that the match is correct, Melissa takes off her headset and rubs her ears. "Sometimes I wonder why they don't just cast people who can sing," she says. "Because synchronizing to someone else's movements isn't easy!"

In fact, however, it's hard to understand why Melissa herself is not playing the role on screen. A slender person, with a mobile, expressive face, Melissa is pretty enough to have been chosen Miss Vermont in a Miss America pageant. But Melissa is rarely seen on camera; she rarely hears the sound of applause. She's known in the pop music business as a studio singer— sometimes called a background singer or a group singer.

What do studio singers do? They are seldom seen but are heard every day. They sing the jingles that sell everything from corn chips to cars. Their voices fill the musical space behind recording stars. They make demonstration tapes so that songwriters can peddle their tunes. They beef up songs on television specials and set the mood as film credits roll. "As well as fill in for movie stars who can't sing," adds Melissa. Occasionally, they are seen as well as heard, but as a backup to the main event, as an added voice behind the star.

"I don't know many people who started out to be studio singers," Melissa says. "I didn't. Most of us wanted to be known. But we're around stars all the time. We see their lives realistically. For me, the burning desire to be famous faded fast."

Nevertheless, Melissa's career as a studio singer began on camera. As Miss Vermont she appeared on the "Tonight" show and sang a duet with Johnny Carson. "To do the show, I had to join the union, the American Federation of Television and Radio Artists (AFTRA)," Melissa explains. "AFTRA's New York policy is to notify members of upcoming auditions. My mailman kept bringing me intriguing postcards." One audition was too intriguing for Melissa to miss.

The call was for a "background singer" for a NBC television show called "The Entertainers." "I had no idea what a background singer did," Melissa says, "but 'The Entertainers' was a favorite show of mine. An incredible number of outstanding performers appeared on it as regulars." Melissa showed up for the audition, along with several hundred others. "The producer in charge of the audition kept saying, 'If you don't read music, don't stay.' I almost left. As it turned out, my sight-reading was more than adequate. They hired one person that day. It was me!"

"The Entertainers" was one of the last "live" shows to be aired on television. It was also one of the last to use background singers on camera. "It was great experience, but it was also cold-shower time. I was thrown into the business as a complete novice."

Melissa watched and learned from the big-name singers who appeared on the show. "Katerina Valenti influenced me tremendously," she says. "She could produce a high sound, yet I knew she wasn't using a head voice. I'm an alto, so my chest voice is most comfortable for me. In college, my teachers tried to bring my head voice down and turn me into a soprano. I felt that was wrong. Katerina warmed up like a trumpet in intervals of fourths and fifths, all from the chest. I took it all in. Now I never use a head voice even though I can hit high C."

From "The Entertainers," Melissa was hired for other television shows in New York and Hollywood. With the promise of more job opportunities, she decided to move west. Soon she was known as one of the most capable studio singers in the Lost Angeles area.

"I'm lucky," she says. "I've never looked for work. It has always come to me."

But luck has little to do with Melissa's success. She possesses certain skills that keep her work in demand. What are they?

Studio singers must be excellent sight-readers. "That's the number one prerequisite." For instance, if Melissa is called to sing the jingle for a shampoo commercial, she is not sent the music in advance of the recording date. Furthermore, on the day of the taping there is no one in the studio to teach her the notes. "Usually, we come in and listen to the accompaniment track, which has been laid down by the musicians in a previous session, to get some idea of the format. Then we read it down a few times—sing the song from top to bottom—and we're ready to tape." Recording studio time is expensive. Every minute costs money. Producers hire singers who have the ability to read music as effortlessly as others read words.

How did Melissa learn to sight-read? "Piano lessons that started when I was very young and continued through high school." Time at the piano is still an important part of her workday. "As I play, I sing along. I constantly work through new musical material."

Second to the ability to sight-read, studio singers must have excellent ears for music. While all singers must possess good ears, studio singers use theirs in a special way. "You've got to listen to what's going on musically and adjust your voice to the sound that is needed," Melissa explains.

For instance, Melissa works frequently with Burt Bacharach. Some of the Bacharach songs she sings are stark and simple, others full and lush. She must quickly "psyche things out" and produce a "fat vibrato" in some places, a "white, pure sound" in others. "Burt hears everything," Melissa says. "So we have to hear everything, too."

Studio singers who get the most calls are versatile. They can sing in a variety of styles and make a variety of sounds. Melissa tells of a studio singer who was asked to show up for a recording session to be a singing chicken. She practiced for hours before the date, locking herself in her room as she tried for the right musical cackling. At last she burst forth. "I can do it! I can do it! I can sing like a chicken!"

Melissa explains that singers with extra abilities are much in demand—singers who can whistle, sing in a foreign language, or mimic unusual sounds.

Studio singers must be willing to be anonymous. Their names are rarely listed on the jackets of albums, even if they've contributed a solo passage or a "step out"—shorter than a solo, usually eight to sixteen bars —to the artist's recording. When they sing a jingle in praise of peanut butter, no one knows whose voice is being heard. And when their behind-the-scenes voices beef up the sound for those appearing on camera, no credit lines list their names at the end of the show.

In fact, when background singers do appear before the public, many disguise themselves as much as possible. "It's a coin toss of a problem," Melissa says. "On one hand, if you appear on camera, say for a commercial, the pay is better. But on the other hand, if your face becomes known, you may work less." The reason? Conflict of interest. A voice can sell three kinds of shampoo with no one the wiser, but an appearance with the product indelibly links the personality with that particular brand.

Even when no product is involved, Melissa takes pains to look different when she appears on camera. "I don't wear a fake nose and dark glasses," she says. "But I do wear wigs so that people watching a television show won't say, 'Hey, isn't that the girl we saw on Dean Martin? Here she is again on Carol Burnett.' "

Anonymity, or lack of stardom, has another valuable plus. Many popular singers find that their careers begin to fade as signs of age touch their faces and bodies. Studio singers, heard but not seen, can have lively careers of long duration if they keep their voices in topnotch shape. One male singer has been singing backgrounds for forty years. No one would guess that his voice is that of a man well past sixty. He keeps his instrument in shape by taking regular lessons, practicing daily, and always warming up fully for recording sessions. But most importantly, he keeps in touch with the latest musical idioms. He can sing the sounds of today as easily as the songs of his youth.

But tonight, Melissa will be seen as well as heard. It's midsummer, and she is appearing at Harrah's Club on the south shore of Lake Tahoe. She is on the road with Burt Bacharach. "Studio singers rarely go out of town," she says, "unless it pays very well. And Burt pays extremely well. He knows he has to, to get us away from our jingles, our accounts."

Harrah's curtain opens to a symphony-sized orchestra arranged on tiers. The music soars as Bacharach strides to his piano. And on the topmost tier, Melissa, along with two other female singers, sits in front of a music rack. When their voices are needed, they stand to sing and then return to their chairs. But at times the stage turns dark, and only the faces of the three women are lit as they "step out" to sing a featured bit. Melissa wears a smartly cut black tuxedo. Her blond hair tumbles around her shoulders. Huge pink-tinted glasses dominate her face. "Burt's show is really a concert," Melissa says. "His lyrics and melodies are so beautiful that stage movement isn't needed. Our voices are like additional instruments in the orchestra."

Three weeks on the road—"It's sort of like a vacation"—and Melissa is back in the recording studios. "Studio singers work hard," she says. "But that's the way I like it. I've made so many recordings that it's hard to remember them all."

She tells of hearing the song "I Am Woman," which rocketed Helen Reddy into stardom, and thinking, "Now, that's a nice tune." Later she learned that her name was listed on a billboard in London along with the names of all the people associated with the hit. "Can you imagine? I'd completely forgotten singing background on it!"

Most of Melissa's calls come from "contractors." Contractors are studio singers who know the performance capabilities and specialties of the studio singers in their area. They put together groups for scheduled recording sessions, set up rehearsals, and aid the producer with the number. They are experts on union contract rules and regulations. Contractors are usually expected to sing with the group they organize. They are paid extra for their contracting services.

What kind of living can a studio singer make? "Good to fantastic," Melissa says. AFTRA sets a minimum scale for each call—as of now $71. If Melissa "steps out" either as a soloist or in a duo for that call, she receives additional pay. If she participates in "multiple tracking"—singing again to the original track to double the sound—she is paid as if each overdub were an additional record side. "I sang a solo Chevron commercial recently," Melissa says. "Not only was the pay extemely good for the taping session, but I receive residual checks every time the commercial is played."

Some jingles are short-lived, others enjoy long plays. Melissa tells of a Coca-Cola commercial she taped with Ray Charles. "Those residual checks came in for years!"

According to industry sources, first-call jingle singers, superstars of the singing commercials who may do as many as ten recording sessions a week, can earn $150,000 a year and more.

The work is seasonal. "Fall to spring, we're busy with new television shows," Melissa says. "Everything is quiet around income tax time—producers must be thinking budget. Summer is slow, so that's when I go on the road. Jingles are pretty much year-round. New York and Los Angeles are the places to be if you really want to get into commercials, while Los Angeles is where the work is for TV."

Melissa is at home, practicing her sight-reading as she accompanies herself on the grand piano that almost fills her living room. It's an often-played piano, not only by Melissa but by her husband, David

Mackay. David, too, is a working musician—a pianist and songwriter with a long list of albums and club dates behind him.

"David is another reason I'm glad to be a studio singer," Melissa says, "because studio singers stay put more than other artists. It's important to me that we can be supportive of each other's career."

David Mackay—curly-haired, lithe, handsome—is blind. Like most of the people Melissa sings for, he has never seen how lovely she is.

11

Songwriter-Singer

Today it is a great advantage to be a songwriter-singer. In recent years, the recording industry has expanded a thousand times over. Hundreds of new studios insatiably gobble up songs for albums and tapes. The demand has never been greater for new material. And this is the age of the personality singers—those who use their voices to express their feelings about life in a highly personal way. No longer is the polished excellence of the voice of prime importance. Instead, it is largely the image projected by the artist that rings up record sales. It's often conceded that the writer may not be the best artist to perform the songs he or she writes, but as a sales pitch, it is usually the most effective.

Kim Carnes's original melodies and lyrics are making her a winner. But right now, Kim is talking about her debut as a recording artist.

"We weren't old enough for drivers' licenses, so we'd find someone to drive us up and down Hollywood's Sunset Boulevard while we looked out of the car windows at recording companies. My best friend and I had been singing regularly for dances at our high school, so we felt we were ready for the big time."

The two girls cased the recording scene in order to decide where best to let their talents be discovered. Finally, gathering courage, they stopped at a likely-looking studio. Kim sat at a piano to play the accompaniment to a song she had written, and they both sang the lyrics.

"The guy in charge said we were great, and if we'd come back that night with $200, he'd make us stars!" With dreams of stardom dancing in their heads, the two girls went home to raise the money: "We promised to wash dishes forever!" Finally with the $200 in hand, the fledgling recording artists returned to the studio. As the man had promised, the tape was made. "As we were leaving," Kim recalls, "he waved and said, 'See you when I come back from Australia. You're first on my list to promote.' "

Six weeks later, with no word from the traveling starmaker, Kim and her friend once again finagled a ride to Sunset Boulevard. The recording company had vanished. In its place was a travel agency.

They had run into an "operator," as such an organization is known in the industry—an unscrupulous, fly-by-night recording company that is in the business of promising young artists stardom in return for cash in advance. Responsible, reputable firms always give proof of what they intend to do before any money changes hands. On request, they make a copy of their contract available for an attorney's evaluation before asking a singer to sign on the dotted line. They are willing to provide an itemized list of the estimated costs of production, a list of the booking agencies with which they work, and evidence that they can handle distribution properly. "Operators" deal with ambiguous contracts or no contracts at all. They make their money by holding out the glittering carrot of stardom.

Kim paid back her parents and grew up enough to carry her own driver's license. But she never stopped singing or writing songs.

"I was writing songs long before I knew it was an advantage to write songs," she says. "As a child, I didn't like to play the tunes assigned by my piano teacher. I liked my own much better. Songwriting is a natural part of my life. I have notebooksful."

Now, in her mid-twenties, Kim records on the A & M label, the company founded by Herb Alpert. It is housed in a rambling, cottage-style plant that was once the studios of comedian Charlie Chaplin. Kim's engaging, husky voice—"I call it 'raspy' "—is of limited range. An excellent musician, she has never tampered with her sound by taking voice lessons. "I like to sing and phrase what comes out naturally," she says. "It would be impossible for me to have someone else tell me how to sing."

The songs she writes, many in collaboration with her husband Dave Ellingson, are largely romantic—about love won, love lost, love savored.

Kim talks about her songs: "Writing is great. You

can just sit down and work every day. Dave and I collaborate well together. I've tried working with others—it's difficult because of egos and inhibitions. You're afraid to say, 'That's awful!' With Dave, if I'm stumped on a song, he'll come in with a fresh new idea.

"Every time I finish a song, I think, 'This is the best one I've ever written.' But you learn to put it aside for a while and then decide if it's the best one you've ever written . . . to wait before you run out and play it for someone. You may be wrong. It may need work. It may not be right for your voice.

"It's exciting to have the whole creative experience of writing a song and then putting it down on a record. But when the taping is finished you always worry. Where will the next song come from? Do I have another in my head?"

All recordings of popular music start with a song. Like Kim, most songwriters work through a publisher. (Many record companies, such as A & M, are also publishers.) And it is usually the publisher who brings songs to the attention of independent record producers and the recording companies' A & R men (Artist and Repertoire men). A & R men match songs with singers and musicians to produce a sound that will make a commercially successful record.

According to Dorene Lauer, West Coast director of publicity at A & M Records, demonstration tapes—"literally boxes of them"—pile up on the A & R man's desk. "Our company hires a guy to take them home and listen to the tons of stuff that come in." What are they listening for? Dorene ponders the question. "How can I define it? Something unique. Something that they can turn people on to."

Cinderella stories are rare in the industry, but occasionally they happen. Dorene Lauer tells of Gino Vannelli, a young rock songwriter-singer. "Gino writes his own material. His music is soulful, sometimes rhythm and blues, sometimes with Latin rhythms. He's a Canadian of Italian descent—so the whole thing makes no sense. Gino pounded on the door here for a long time with no response. Then one day one of Gino's friends sneaked past the guard at the gate, burst into Herb Alpert's office, literally threw a demonstration tape on his desk, said, 'Listen to this!' and ran out. Finally, Gino's stuff was heard. And it was good. Gino Vannelli records regularly for us now and is well on his way to a fantastic career. But a success story like his is rare, very rare."

Dorene goes on to say that Gino was not really plucked out of obscurity and plunked down into stardom. Gino Vannelli has been singing, performing, and writing songs since he was twelve.

How did Kim's voice and songs find their way through the deluge of material on the A & R man's desk? She worked her way in. For many years she steadily built a reputation, not with the general public but with people in the industry.

"I made demos—demonstration tapes—first as a favor for songwriter friends who were not singers and then for publishing companies. I sang a lot of songs in a lot of styles in a lot of studios. My voice was all over the industry. The right people began to know me. Success is largely a matter of whom you know."

"No!" Dorene quickly shakes her head. "It's what the people you know know about you!"

Kim Carnes's reputation is that of an excellent, flexible songwriter-singer who is knowledgeable about theory, arranging, and composition. She is known to be reliable in meeting deadlines and commitments. And her voice and songs possess the looked-for elusive quality of salable uniqueness. All of these are important qualities for success.

Singers and songwriters peddle their wares with demos. Kim tells how the demonstration tapes are made: "It's usually just piano and voice. Sometimes I do a harmony part with myself on an added track. There are two demo philosophies—some go in and make almost a finished product because they want the producer to hear the full impact of how the song will sound. Others give as little as possible so that the producer can use his imagination and envision how he would make the record. Neither way has been proven best. I go back and forth between them.

"A taping in a professional studio can cost $100 or thousands of dollars. It's a good idea not to spend too much. Dave and I do our demos at home. We've bought a four-track machine, so now our only cost is the price of tape."

Kim's first album for A & M, *Kim Carnes* is in the stores. No hit single from the recording has pushed its way up the charts to ensure spectacular album sales. "But it's getting good play," Kim says. A second album is in the works. Cost of the first album: around $50,000.

A recording company acts like a patron. "The company supports the artist so that he or she can produce the art," Dorene explains. "But of course we both stand to make a profit. We're here to sell records for an artist. We advance the money, press the record, package and promote the product. After the money advanced is recouped from sales, the artist begins to get checks from royalties."

Now Kim is on the road, playing the opening act for headliner Neil Sedaka. A & M is paying the bills for the tour, knowing that personal appearances stimulate record sales.

"Except for a tour with the New Christy Minstrel Singers a few years ago, my experience is all studio," Kim says. "But I love to perform, to get feedback from an audience."

Kim appears on stage in blue jeans—"I have a few special tops I like to wear." She plays the piano for a couple of numbers and tells quiet stories about a lyric —"whatever comes into my head." Backed by musicians who are all friends—Dave plays one guitar—her performances are comfortable and casual. Audiences are responsive, reviews favorable. From *Variety*, dateline New York, March 17: "Kim Carnes, as is her custom on her A & M records, does mostly originals . . . she convinced an aud which was waiting for the headliner but became hers for a solid half-hour or more. . . . A dynamite-looking blond, Carnes is a good singer who really gets into a lyric, though at times, on a few up numbers early, she seemed to be holding back a bit. Once she turned it all loose, though, it completely captivated the audience. She'll be back."

Kim went to Muscle Shoals, Alabama, to turn out her second album for A & M. Why Muscle Shoals and not the rambling studio complex in Hollywood? First of all, Hollywood and Tin Pan Alley no longer monopolize the recording industry. Today there are major music and recording centers across America—Seattle, San Francisco, Bakersfield, Denver, Chicago, Detroit, Philadelphia, Cincinnati, Nashville, Memphis, Atlanta, Macon, Jackson, Dallas, Austin, Houston, New Orleans, Miami, and Muscle Shoals, as well as Los Angeles and New York.

"My producer likes to work in Muscle Shoals," Kim says. "And I can see why. Muscle Shoals is a small community surrounded by open country. Eight recording studios are in town. Here we'll do the album in two weeks, in one concentrated effort. In Hollywood you work on it, take time off, back on it again. Hollywood's musicians are incredibly good, but they may have done three other sessions that day before they get to yours. Here, the musicians are just as good, but they work on one project at a time. Nothing much but recording goes on in Muscle Shoals. It's quiet, no distractions. You can just work."

Once Kim has recorded one of her original songs, anyone else is free to use it as long as they register their use with the publishing company. "Then I'm paid royalties," Kim says. If someone wants a song that has not been recorded, they must be licensed by the publishing company to do so. "My philosophy used to be, my songs for me to record first. But I no longer feel that way. If a top artist has my song coming out and I have it coming out, too, that's a nice situation to be in. If someone has a hit on my song, how can I lose!"

≡12≡

Country and Western

A bale of hay, a wagon wheel, and blowin' on a jug. That's what country music used to be. But a quiet revolution has been going on in Nashville in recent years. Strings, horns, and keyboards have joined the steel guitars and fiddles to produce a new sound that is closer to rock, closer to jazz, closer to pop ballads, but is still unmistakably country.

Recently the County Music Association, an industrywide association organized to promote country music, spent a great deal of time trying to come up with a definition of what a country song was. They gave up. They should have simply asked Kris Kristofferson. "If it sounds like country, man it's country," he says.

In Nashville, the undisputed capital of country

music, a cross section of every kind of American music parades across the Grand Ole Opry stage—pop, rock 'n' roll, honky-tonk, bluegrass, spirituals, rhythm and blues. Country music borrows from all of it, but one basic ingredient never changes. The song is always a story, told simply, of people trying to get along in the world the best they can.

"More than any other kind of music, country gets down a little deeper into real-life emotions, real heartbreak, real joys and sorrows," explains Eddie Rabbitt, a young Nashville songwriter-singer. "It spells out a little closer to home people's everyday troubles in their work, marriages and relationships with others."

Right now, Eddie Rabbitt's "Two Dollars in the Juke Box" is spinning its way up the country charts toward number one. And he's delighted. But Eddie's music did not suddenly plunk out of his guitar and pop on to the best-selling charts. He's traveled a long, hard country music road to become today's hottest thing in Nashville.

"Scratch a country singer and somewhere you'll find a fiddle," says one authority on the music. The fiddle in Eddie's background belonged to his Irish-born father, who played the Irish dance halls in New York City. "There was always lots of music in our house," Eddie remembers. He adds that one of his earliest memories was as a small child sitting at the dining room table with company present for dinner. One of the guests asked the usual question adults put to children: "What are you going to be when you grow up?" Without hesitation Eddie answered, "A singer." And today he says, "That's what I wanted to be then, and that's what I want to be now. I've never given a whole lot of thought to any other kind of job."

Eddie discovered country music in the Boy Scouts. He explains: "Our scoutmaster happened to be a country singer who played the clubs in New Jersey. One weekend we were out on a hike, and he pulled out this jumbo guitar and started playing some stuff. I fell in love with the sound of it." Eddie asked his scoutmaster to teach him to play. "He taught me three chords, C, G, and F, and then moved away."

So, at the age of twelve, Eddie began to work at his life's goal in the great tradition of country music—he taught himself to play. With few exceptions, country artists are self-taught, self-made musicians. Nevertheless, they are known as some of the most able in the business.

"I went to downtown Newark and bought myself a little guitar book," Eddie says, continuing his story. "And I just went through that book learning the chords, then looking at sheet music trying to match up my fingers with the songs." He didn't know how to read music. "I took piano lessons for a while when I was younger, and my teacher had me try to read, but I didn't like it. It was too much like arithmetic." What he was interested in was the feel, the emotion, rather than trying to figure out dotted eights and sixteenths.

Later he returned to the piano—"I picked it up myself." He also taught himself to play drums and bass— "I play them kind of hairy-like, but I get by." When he got his guitar chords down pat, he spent the next few years playing and singing around his neighborhood— "at parties and this and that."

It is often said of country artists that their lives reflect the themes of their music. One manager says, "Country people don't have much flair to their lives, and they go through their careers like it is life. Their careers are real, not phony."

In Eddie's sophomore year in high school, his life began to take on the stark realism of the lyrics of the songs he sang. His parents divorced, his family scattered, and he quit school. "I lied about my age and went upstate New York to work as an orderly in a mental hospital," he says. His guitar made the move, too. He sang at parties and dances for the patients. One performance was particularly memorable: "I was singing some Elvis Presley songs and I was sounding pretty good, and the band we'd got together was sounding pretty good. The patients began to shout, 'Elvis! Elvis!' It was an interesting experience signing autographs and all."

Soon after, Eddie left his job at the mental hospital —"I was beginning to feel too comfortable there"— and returned to New Jersey to play odd jobs while he went to night school to earn his high school diploma.

At graduation time, he and some friends dropped by a neighborhood club, the Six Steps Down. "The owner and the piano player were in the middle of a big argument," Eddie recalls. "Finally the piano player had enough, got up, and walked out." That exit marked Eddie's entrance into the professional country music business. The next night he had a shot at the job. "I got up there with my little electric guitar and my little amplifier and my music stand." The music stand held the lyrics to all the country recordings he knew how to play. "I wasn't into memorizing every single word to every single song. So I stayed up late the night before and copied them all on to pieces of paper. It worked pretty good."

It worked more than good. Business at the Six Steps Down boomed, and two more musicians joined Eddie. They became a band. "We were getting a reputation around town," Eddie says. For the next couple of years they were the highest-paid and most-in-demand country group in the area. But Eddie grew restless. "I was tired of going around in circles. I wanted to be a star." And he was pretty sure the road to country stardom was paved with original songs.

As the Country Music Association explains, Eddie was right. Recording companies are reluctant to sign nonwriting newcomers because they are concerned that they will lack material to sing. Established writers want established stars to sing their songs, stars whose popularity might propel their tunes into million-sales markets. A would-be recording artist who can also write topnotch music and lyrics has a better chance of landing a contract.

What makes a topnotch tune? Originality. If a song is to catch the ear of a publisher, and eventually the listening public, it must be fresh and new. It must be different in idea, lyric, and melody from any other written.

Once a song is written, the next step is to submit the song to music publishers. Usually this is done by sending demo tapes along with typewritten copies of the lyric to publishing companies. Lists of reputable publishers can be gotten from BMI (Broadcast Music,

Inc.) and ASCAP (American Society of Composers, Authors, and Publishers), the two performing rights societies that license publishers and pay writers for radio and television performance of their tunes.

But Eddie peddled his first songs in a slightly different way. "I put my twelve best original tunes on tape, just me playing the guitar and singing," he explains. "Then I took out my *Country Song Round Up*—a monthly magazine that prints words for the pickers out there who need lyrics to the songs they hear on the radio. At the bottom of each lyric a credit line lists the names and addresses of the publisher of that song."

The day before Eddie caught the bus to New York, he called twelve publishers from the credit lines in *Country Song Round Up*. "I have some songs. I'd like to come in and play them for you." Twelve appointments were made.

"I was real dumb in those days." Eddie chuckles. "I took a fifty-pound tape recorder with me on the bus and carried it white-knuckled all over New York. It was a heavy dude! It never occurred to me that the publishers would have tape recorders in their offices."

He was turned down, "colder than ice," on eleven calls. His last appointment was with a big company with a country division called Painted Desert. "They took my tape and said, 'Come back in an hour and we'll tell you what we think.' So I walked around, came back in an hour, and was called into an office and then into another office and down the hall and into another office. I thought, 'Maybe something's shaking here!' "

Something *was* shaking. Painted Desert believed

that Eddie's tunes showed exceptional talent, talent that needed to be—"I'll never forget the words," Eddie says—"polished and groomed."

Eddie was lucky. He signed with a reputable publisher. Many publishers are not. Inexperienced writers should be aware that the first clue that they may be dealing with an unscrupulous publisher is a request for money. Unscrupulous publishers want to be paid ahead to look at a song, to set the music to lyrics or the lyrics to music, to publish and promote. Many new songwriters, eager to be published at any price, sign on the dotted line. An honest publisher assumes all costs for publication, distribution, and promotion.

Eddie polished and groomed his talent for a year at Painted Desert, drawing a weekly salary from the publishing company. "I probably wrote a hundred songs—all just this side of being right on."

His contract up with Painted Desert, Eddie returned to New Jersey to work the clubs. "I was awful tired of the same old thing. I had more ambition than to end up in Newark, New Jersey. I told my band, 'Nothing's going to happen here. I'm going to Nashville. Any of you guys going to come?' But they weren't ready for that big, irresponsible move."

Once again, his career began to resemble the lyrics of a country song. He hopped on a Greyhound bus headed for Nashville. "I checked into one of the fleabags downtown and sat soaking in the bathtub, washing the bus off my body. I watched the water go down the drain and thought, 'What happens when you hit bottom and then the bottom falls out?' " The title came first, "Working My Way Up to the Bottom."

"Titles have a musical sound when you say them over and over," he says. "They have a little melody that flows out with the thought."

He got out of the tub and picked up his guitar to find the chords to the tune he was singing "Pretty soon I got a little format going, a little shell for the song." "Working My Way Up to the Bottom," recorded by a major country artist, was to be his first successful "cut."

Things started shaking for Eddie in Nashville. A second song, "Bottles," was cut by another established artist. The lyrics told how bottles affect people's lives —first the baby bottle, then soda bottles, and finally a bottle of poison that ends it all. "It was a sick little tune," Eddie says, "but it went to about thirty on the Hit Parade."

To show his songs around, Eddie made what he calls "funky garage-type demos." He invested in a sound-on-sound tape recorder and added drum, bass, and harmonies to his voice and guitar. "They sounded pretty good and gave a better rendition of the idea I was trying to get across, but still left enough room for a producer's imagination."

Because most country music is a story told simply, guitar-vocal demos are usually considered sufficient to show what a song has to offer. "This is changing a bit as country gets more and more mixed up with rock and other kinds of music," Eddie comments. "But basically it's enough to tape the song and the singer and not add on a whole lot of electric, heavy metal stuff to sell it."

He signed a five-year contract with a Nashville publishing company. "I came to Nashville to become a singing star, but it took me a while to get the writer-singer breakdown clear in my head. Finally, I woke up to the fact that no big writer was going to give me his hit song. I also figured that my voice alone was not going to knock a recording company flat. Recording deals are hard to come by. I was already a singer. Now I had to knuckle down and become a good writer. I'd work at it until my songs would be so great that everyone would be after them. And then I'd say, 'Only if you record them on me can you have them.' "

Again Eddie "polished and groomed." Elvis Presley recorded three of his songs. One, "Kentucky Rain," hit a million sales. More top artists cut his tunes. "I was fortunate. Everyone in the business was recording my music."

Eddie's contract with the publishing company guaranteed him a salary of $37.50 a week. "I lived on that until the money from my songs started coming in."

Songwriters' money comes from two sources—over-the-counter record sales and pay for play. "But in country, you don't make a whole lot of money over the counter," Eddie explains. "Unlike pop hits that sell a million records, a country hit is 100,000 sold. At a penny a record, that's only $1,000."

The big money comes from radio play. Every time a writer's tune is spun on the air, the station must pay from two to six cents into a fund held by ASCAP or BMI. The writer splits that money with his publisher. It's not unusual for a good record to be played across the country 75,000 to 80,000 times. That number multiplied by the few pennies paid for each play turns a tidy profit.

Eddie returns to his story: "A friend in the business made some free recording time available to me. I wanted to see how my tunes would sound if I took them out of the garage and into the studio. We put down guitar-vocals and then asked some musician friends to come in to overdub drums and bass. It started to sound pretty good. One day, a guy named Mike Settle from Elektra Records dropped by and just fell out. 'We've gotta have you, boy!' he said."

Eddie's polishing and grooming days were over. His first singing single, "You Get to Me," went to seventeen on the *Billboard* charts. (*Billboard* is a weekly publication that keeps track of what is happening in the recording industry.) His second, "Forgive and Forget," moved up to twelve. Single number three, "I Should Have Married You," climbed to number eleven. And the fourth, "Drinking My Baby off My Mind," hit the top at number one. "Rocky Mountain Music" and "Two Dollars in the Juke Box" followed suit—across the board at number one. And that's when Nashville said, "The kid's the hottest thing on the streets!"

Eddie is ready to run with his dream. "I'll try out a new manager every day of the week until I find one who's into promoting me twenty-four hours a day. My dream is coming true, and I'm putting it in someone else's hands! I'm not about to let anyone drop my dream and let it splatter. Right now I'm in a place where I'll never be again. Never again will I be young, hot, and happening. If we lose it now, let it cool down even a bit, I won't be new any more. You go downhill and you come up old."

Eddie and his band—"drum, bass, steel guitar, piano, lead guitar, and me"—are hitting the road with a management behind them that is "promoting explosions all over the place." Newspaper ads, interviews, television and radio spots, "posters on the telephone poles" let his fans know that he is coming to town. An agent has booked them into places "where we can reflect our biggest shine."

It is a Thursday night in 1978, and the thirteenth annual Academy of Country Music Awards is underway. "And now, the award for the top new male vocalist. The envelope, please. Eddie Rabbitt!"

So far, it's Eddie Rabbitt's biggest shine. He is young, hot, and happening.

≡13≡

Jazz Song Stylist

Madeline Eastman is bucking the tide. At a time when the pop music industry is gobbling up original material at a record rate, she does not write songs. At a time when publicity departments package performers for the idolization of their fans, Madeline appears as Madeline. At a time when the personal statement made by the song is considered more important than the quality of the voice stating it, Madeline uses her voice with artistry and control.

Madeline, although she knows her kind of music is not hot in today's marketplace, is a stylist of other people's songs. Her style? Jazz.

Before rock 'n' roll hit the music scene, song stylists were what pop music was all about. To sing well was to entertain. Today, Madeline Eastman is totally involved in singing well. A phrase is stretched just so. A note is bent but arrives at its destination precisely on time and in tune. To Madeline, words are important,

118

whether coming lickety-split in a jabberwocky jive tune or flowing smoothly in a torchy ballad. She is constantly polishing and perfecting her style.

"When I saw the movie *Lady Sings the Blues*, with Diana Ross playing the jazz singer Billie Holiday, something clicked," Madeline says. "I *knew* I should be a singer. Before that, I *felt* I should be a singer. Inside I *felt* something when I sang. My voice wasn't particularly good. I wasn't one of the star students in our high school choir. But, how can I explain it—I just *felt* something!

"My voice was weak, I couldn't hold a note, my range was small, but when I saw that movie, I *knew* I should be a singer."

Madeline heard of a retired jazz singer and went to her for lessons. "There I discovered that what I *felt* couldn't come out of my mouth for a very simple reason—I was scared. We worked together for a year, not on technique, but on opening my powers of communication."

Communication is the song stylist's stock in trade. Great stylists like Frank Sinatra, Peggy Lee, and Tony Bennett have the ability to make their listeners believe that right now, at this very instant, for the very first time, they have discovered the intimate magic of the song they are singing.

While Madeline developed her power to communicate what she felt, she learned vocal technique on her own. "There were certain things that I wanted my voice to be able to do. So I listened to recordings by singers who could do those things. I had every album made by the great jazz singer Carmen McRae. I sang along with Carmen verbatim. I practiced with her over and over again. She was the best teacher! Carmen McRae's phrasing, which I admired and copied, is part of me now and creeps into everything I sing."

Madeline also sang along with recordings cut by jazz horn soloists. "When you sing a horn part, your voice learns to go all over the place. It takes months and months to get one of those songs to where you can hit all the pitches." Horn solos, like Lester Young's "Jazz Jump" and Miles Davis's "Four," with lyrics added, are now part of Madeline's repertoire.

"When you sing a horn solo, the whole point is to exactly duplicate what the horn plays. Only very subtle changes in interpretation or phrasing occur. The effect is improvisational, but actually the piece is learned in a careful way."

Madeline pauses and then adds, "But I've heard some people sing those horn solos, and while they hit all the notes, somehow it isn't right. The song doesn't get off the ground."

What she is talking about is an innate ability to project rhythm that is more than a beat, to know when to bend the time, how to attack a note, how to phrase a song for the greatest impact. "That's the difference between the greats and the nobodies with the beautiful voices," she sums up. "And that difference is something that can't be taught."

Madeline enrolled in college as a music major. "But I dropped out. It was too classical, not applicable to what I knew I should do. What good would it do to stand there for four years with my hands clasped singing " 'Hark, Hark the Lark'?"

She went to work in a neighborhood café, the Owl and the Monkey. "A guitarist and I sat on little two-foot-high stools and were paid about four dollars a night to sing and play." Although the Owl and the Monkey barely paid enough to buy her supper, it gave her an opportunity to try out new material and develop her charts.

Charts are musical maps. They diagram the chord changes of a particular song in the singer's key. Charts are the bare bones of the music—musicians are expected to fill in the spaces between the chord changes. Charts are indispensable to singers like Madeline, who work from club to club, often with different musicians each night.

More times than not, Madeline meets the particular combination of players for the first time when she shows up for that night's work. Seldom is there opportunity for rehearsal.

"Believe it or not, that's an advantage," she says. "Every time the song sounds different because whoever is on the bass, drum, guitar, vibes, piano, or whatever is doing what he feels should go on between the basic chord changes. It keeps me on my toes; I never know what's going to happen. It's really fun! Scary at first, but fun! Now I've worked enough to have confidence that it will all work out."

It's Thursday night at Shenanigans, the dimly lit, casual downtown listening club where Madeline has been singing for the past few weeks. She flips through a looseleaf binder filled with her alphabetized charts to "call" to the band her next number. "Shenanigans is a loose and friendly place. I don't plan out the whole performance in advance. Instead, I listen to the audience's response and then decide what to do next."

As if they have played together forever, Madeline and the band move into Gershwin's "Fascinating Rhythm," full of precise stop-start breaks and sophisticated syncopation. "I work with fantastic musicians. When I first began to sing two years ago, I heard, starry-eyed, about the people I play with today. To know that now those same musicians treat me as an equal gives me a great sense of progression in my career."

Now, eyes shut, hands clasped on mike, head thrown slightly back, Madeline turns her entire attention to a ballad. Totally involved with the song, she attempts no interpretative gestures or facial expressions. Without fuss, she works as if her voice were another instrument in the band.

"I don't involve myself with the audience as much as I should," she says, discussing what she considers to be a fault in her performance. If it is a fault, it is one shared with many great stylists who consider the music more important than between-song chatter or visual dramatization of the song. "When I first started to sing, I never opened my eyes—never, ever. Now, at least, I can get them open at times and try to get an appropriate expression on my face that reflects the lyrics. But the truth is that while I'm singing, I'm conscious only of the song. I could be anywhere. But the moment I stop, I think, 'Oh, yeah. Here I am.' And I become very aware of the audience's reaction. At that moment I feel terribly self-conscious, manage to say thank you, and schlepp off to the side of the stage to confer with the band about our next tune.

"At Shenanigans, that's okay because it's a casual place. But it's a goal of mine to not deny the audience. The audience has a right to expect a bit of showmanship from me—to at least chat about the upcoming tune and fill in the space while the band gets its charts up for the next song. Oh, that's hard for me to do—horrible! Let me sing—don't make me talk!"

Madeline is playing The City, a sophisticated uptown club with a stage, professional light and sound men, and a master of ceremonies who announces, "And now, ladies and gentlemen, Madeline Eastman." She steps to the mike, dressed, as one critic later reported, like a St. Laurent model. The audience is seated at tables, not milling about as at the Shenanigan's bar. Madeline has their complete attention. Ballads are spun out to a whisper, not lost in the clink of glasses and talk.

For this engagement, charts have been expanded into complete arrangements—it has not been left to chance what improvisations will occur between chord changes. The same musicians will be on hand for the entire run at The City. Madeline has worked out lines of patter that tie her songs together. Tonight there will be no leafing through the charts in search of the next number. Madeline Eastman is a polished act.

One critic's review began, "Last night I heard a singer . . . the young Madeline Eastman, only two years of singing behind her but a voice and manner that predict a lifetime of professional success."

Madeline talks of the impact of that review: "That was my first, my one and only, review. When I found out that a critic had been there, I wanted to die. I thought I'd be crucified! After I got up the courage to find out what had been said, I ran out and bought about fourteen stacks of that edition and mimeographed the review a thousand times. What the critic said made me feel legitimate. He told me, 'Madeline, you are a singer.' The review also opened doors for work at some of the nicer jazz clubs."

The market for Madeline's songs is limited. Jobs where listening music is wanted are far from plentiful. There is much more work available for pop singers who can supply music for dancing crowds. Madeline turns down those offers. "I'm a jazz stylist. That's what I'm good at . That's what I do."

Madeline sits cross-legged on the floor of her living room. A Carmen McRae record plays softly in the background. She talks about what should happen next. "A good publicity photo, for sure." And a manager— "There aren't many around who understand jazz singers." More dates in small clubs "to work out new material." More concerts "where people really listen." And then New York City—"As it has always been, that's where great jazz lives."

Madeline feels the tide is turning: "I'm lucky to be blossoming now." There seems evidence of increased interest in her kind of song. For the time being, Madeline is happy producing jazz anywhere, in clubs big or small. Without a shadow of a doubt, she *knows* she should be a singer.

=14=

Rock 'n' Roll

In the mid-fifties, rock 'n' roll burst upon the pop scene. The established music industry gasped at the raucous, rip-it-up sounds but decided to hold its breath until rock would roll away. But the high-decibel, high-energy music was not to be ignored. Today, rock 'n' roll is a two-billion-dollar industry that has catapulted record companies into the category of big business. It has also influenced the attitudes of a generation and a half of listeners. Rock 'n' roll to most fans is more than music. It symbolizes a way of life.

No wonder that in garages all over the country, hundreds of would-be rock artists are tuning up their guitars and turning up their amplifiers in the hope of breaking into the action. Some of the most talented and most original will make it to the top.

Not long ago, the rock trio known as Jelly was perfecting its act on the fringes of the industry. Then the big business of rock cracked open for the group. Today they are on their way.

Right now Amy Madigan, the female one-third of Jelly, is describing the rock group's first road experience—a national tour of twenty-one gigs (performances) in twenty-five days that came hard on the heels of Jelly's first album release, "A True Story," recorded by Elektra-Asylum records. Reviews were good, a hit single hoped for, and the record company sent them out to ride the publicity generated by their recording.

"I love to tour!" Amy speaks in a slightly gravelly voice that seems to be on a perpetual binge of enthusiasm. "I love to check into a different motel every day. I love to play the gig, pack up, get in the bus, and move on. We got to Phoenix and I said, 'Hey, it's great to be here in Denver.' By that time I didn't know or care where we were!

"Our first gig was before 10,000 people," she continues, "and I couldn't wait to get out there. 'Get that spotlight on me!' If I'd had to stand up and give a lecture or something, I'd have been scared. But I was with Jelly. I was with my team. It was terrific!"

Then Amy's mood swings abruptly. "But it was hard, too. People hadn't come to see Freddy, Jesse, and me. They'd come to see the headliner, Bread. We were lucky if people were even sitting down."

Concert headliners play anywhere from an hour to three hours a performance. Opening acts are lucky if a half-hour of playing time is alloted to them. They choose carefully from their repertoire to put together a powerhouse set that will show their stuff in those few minutes.

Opening acts often share the concert bill with three or four other support groups—all there for the purpose of warming up the audience for the big-name head-liner the audience paid their money to see.

"We had thirty-five minutes on the Bread tour," Amy says. "And each time it was over, I'd count the minutes until I could do it again."

A national tour for Jelly before audiences of 10,000 was a big step in a short time from their regular gig at the Bla-Bla Cafe, a small club that holds seventy peo-ple packed to the walls. There Jesse Roe, Fred Blif-fert, and Amy worked on and off for a year and a half as a rock trio.

Amy tells Jelly's story: "A cab driver came in one night and said, 'I really like you guys. I'm going to bring in a fellow who has some contacts.' Now, if I had a nickel for every time someone told me they were bringing some big guy in, I'd have my own bank. So I said, 'Sure, sure.'

"Then late one night we were into the fourth set with about three people in the place, just getting down and having fun, when this gray-haired weirdo came in, sat down, and really started moving around. We played to this guy for about a half-hour."

Amy's gray-haired "weirdo" was the cab driver's contact, a producer from Elektra-Asylum records. The group was on its way to a recording contract. It was also suddenly big business.

Rock groups always start out as a handful of compatible musicians who make good sounds together. If they become successful, they end up surrounded by an entourage of experts who are expected to take care of the complexities of the rock business, freeing the performers to do what they do best—make music.

Managers, lawyers, agents, accountants, roadies (the people responsible for the packing and setting up of equipment), lighting men, sound experts, publicists —all smooth the way for successful gigs. They also take a percentage from the earnings—10 percent or more for managers and agents, a negotiable percentage or salary for the rest.

Other expenses take their cut: publicity photos, transportation (whether it be by dusty station wagon, specially outfitted bus, or Elton John-style Starship), hotels, meals, demo tapes, arrangers, backup musicians, stage clothes, business gifts, telephone bills, answering service, equipment and instruments, and insurance for them, union dues to AFM (the American Federation of Musicians) and AFTRA (the American Federation of Television and Radio Artists), social security payments, and state and local taxes.

But if all goes well with the group, the money will come rolling in: income from live and television appearances, record company advances, royalties on record sales, publishing royalties, along with ASCAP or BMI accountings of record play.

For some stars, rock 'n' roll is here to pay. At least thirty-five individuals and fifteen groups earn between two and six million dollars a year. Their money comes from fans, mostly between the ages of twelve and thirty-two, who shell out two billion dollars a year for records and tapes and another 150 million dollars to see their favorites in concert.

Jelly is not numbered among the million-dollar star groups, but they plan to be.

What does it take? "Most people have the idea that luck makes stars," says Allen Shapiro, Jelly's manager-lawyer—not an unusual combination in the legally complex record-rock industry. "They're fortunate, perhaps, but not lucky. What it takes is persistence and talent."

Amy says bluntly, "Overnight successes? That's a lot of bull."

As a small child, Amy knew she wanted some part of stardom. "And my parents said, 'Go to it!' They were entirely supportive."

She badgered her parents for a piano—"Finally, when I was seven, they bought me one"—and studied classical piano for ten years. She was also exposed to musicians and music of all kinds. "My brother, the jazz freak, used to sneak me into clubs. My parents would say, 'You're not going to school today—Horowitz is in town.' I saw the greats at a young age.

"Voice lessons? No! I was the kid who from age five on was out there buying records. I'd go up to my room and listen, memorize the words, imitate the singer, invent harmonies if there were none. If there were harmonies, like on the old Beach Boy songs that have tons of parts, I'd pick them out and learn them all.

"No one knew I sang," Amy continues. "In high school, since I played piano, I accompanied everyone else."

At Wisconsin's Marquette University, Amy enrolled

as a philosophy major. "Well, actually I enrolled in rock 'n' roll and went to college when I had time. There, I met these three guys and they said, 'We're looking for a chick singer'—a term I abhor! And I said, 'I sing.' Oh, I lied. Said I'd sung in this band and that. They said, 'We have a gig tomorrow night.' I said, 'Great!' So, at age seventeen—I'd never sung outside my room—I went to play the gig. I was pretty good! Winging it entirely. Not a bit scared. I'd been ready a long time."

Soon her path crossed Jesse Roe's, who now is keyboard player and songwriter for Jelly. Jesse studied piano for five years during his teens. "I also amassed an astounding collection of about four hundred R and B (rhythm and blues) singles that I listened to constantly." In high school, Jesse formed a soul-flavored band, The Messengers. Then Jesse enrolled at Marquette and at the same time studied composition at the University of Wisconsin.

"While going to college, I played keyboards and sang and composed material for an outrageous band, Methyl Ethyl and the Keytones." When the band needed a drummer, they called in one, who brought along his girl friend, Amy Madigan. "Three weeks later," Jesse recalls, "the drummer left, and we kept Amy as lead vocalist."

Amy picks up the story. "We practiced and played seven days a week, rehearsing in a house on the east side of Milwaukee. We wrote all our own material. We were into weirdness, offending and shocking the audience. People hated us. They threw things at me and yelled, 'Get off the stage!' We thought we were so cool!"

Methyl Ethyl and the Keystones played its last discordant note, and Amy was invited to join a country-rock band, the Hound Dog Band, formed by Fred Bliffert, who is now vocalist-guitarist with Jelly.

Fred organized his first band the Freeloaders, when he was a sophomore in high school. But he really wanted to be an actor. For a while he hosted a Milwaukee television show and played parts in a local theater group, at the same time performing with Freddy (named after himself) and the Freeloaders. Finally, the Freeloaders disbanded, and Fred's Hound Dog Band, with Amy as lead vocalist, took up where the Freeloaders left off. The Hound Dogs toured extensively through the Midwest and then broke up.

The time seemed right for Amy to get into her VW and head for Los Angeles. "My plan? To make it in this business." She talks of those first hard months in the rock capital of the world. "You beat the streets. You audition for lousy people. You read the newspaper classifieds that advertise for singers. And there's a thing out here called Musicians Contact Service that puts you together with people looking for singers. I worked with a lot of bands, with little chance for rehearsal. But I was good. I can jump into a situation and do it. I'm a professional."

When work grew steady, Amy contacted Fred and Jesse. "I said, 'Get on out here!'" The two men met for the first time in Los Angeles. Jelly was born at the Bla-Bla Cafe, and the rock trio began to develop its own sound.

Groups that hit the top are innovators, not imitators. They work for a sound that is distinctively their own, not a copycat version of an admired headliner. Funky, soft and sweet, or freaky, heavy acid rock—each group must decide what it wants its sound to be.

"The first thing we found out working as a trio," Jesse says, "was that we needed an identity—an identifiable style, an identifiable sound. And that was difficult because we all like everything!"

But one thing was certain—the crazy psychotic songs that outraged Wisconsin audiences were no longer effective. "One day it dawned on us," Jesse says, "that, hey, this doesn't work. It doesn't move audiences. It's not appealing. When we do other kinds of songs, people like us better. They're more receptive to our message."

Jesse, Fred, and Amy found a common vein in the sounds and style of rhythm and blues. The word went around that Jelly was worth listening to.

The group also worked on the development of original material. Until the Beatles and Bob Dylan made their impact on the pop music scene, performers didn't write their own songs. It was considered enough that an artist be a stylist, an interpreter of someone else's musical message.

Today, most rock bands write at least half their own songs. And when they include another artist's hit in their sets, they know that a mere duplication of the original rendition is not enough. They must either do the song better or give it fresh meaning with a new approach to style and sound.

Right now, there are literally hundreds of groups

jockeying for a piece of the rock action. The production of bright, meaningful original material is perhaps the most important way for any one of them to stand out as a tree in the forest of rock 'n' roll.

"Do you want to hear the same song over and over again?" Amy asks. "I know that I don't want to keep singing one that's been recorded over and over again by other people. That's no good.

"So Fred and Jesse write new stories for Jelly, and I help tell them—happy, sad, goofy, whatever. That's my job. And I tell stories better than anyone I know. Does that sound presumptuous? Well, it's presumptuous to go up on stage. You'd better have something to say. I may not be the greatest singer in the world. But, oh, do I care about the words." Amy sings them in a voice that can be enormous, purring, husky, shouting, torchy—whatever is needed to tell Jelly's tales.

Persistence, solid musicianship, an identifiable sound, original material that expresses a message—all help to pave the way to the top. But one other element is essential—the ability to hold together through bad times as well as good.

Rock groups are notorious for splitting up, forming and re-forming as rapidly as amoebas under a microscope. Many split out of existence. Those that remain work hard to maintain their spirit, sound, and style regardless of the comings and goings of musicians. Holding the group together is an all-important, never-ending goal. It means the difference between success and failure.

Jelly's basic identity is a three-person team: Jesse on piano, Amy as lead singer and occasional player of the glockenspiel, castanets, and vibraphonette—"crazy percussion stuff"—and Fred, who takes his turn at telling his stories and fills in with guitar. All three sing backup to each other.

The rock trio's basic vocal-combo-with-piano sound was sufficient to fill the Bla-Bla Cafe. But it wasn't rich enough for the recording sessions at Elektra-Asylum. And it wasn't enough to carry a gig for an audience of 10,000. It was obvious that Jelly would have to bring in new musicians and become an electric band. Amy, Fred, and Jesse worried about the impact of additional instruments. Might it clutter up Jelly's clean sound? "Overnight we had a sax, a bass, guitar, drum—the whole works," Amy says. "The miracle is that we pulled it off without destroying our identity."

With the record and the tour behind them, the three pulled back to their tightly knit team. "Oh, sometimes we fight," Amy admits with glee. "I scream at Jesse and Fred. We yell at each other. Man, we get in fights! So what! You only fight with people you care about." Jelly is a unit that has held together through thick and thin. Together they keep plugging away with spirit and determination to be numbered among the best.

"We'll add musicians again, I'm sure," Amy goes on to explain. "But right now, we're locked into the three of us so that we can get our material down." They are back at the Bla-Bla Cafe, where they can hear feedback from the audience—"to find out what works, what doesn't work"—in preparation for their next album, their next gig on the road.

As with all groups, constant rehearsal makes the material work.

Beginning groups practice wherever they can find space—usually in garages and living rooms until the neighbors complain. Rehearsal studios, found in the yellow pages or by word of mouth, charge from five to fifty dollars an hour. Studios furnish or rent PA systems, amplifiers, and microphones—it's a big expense, but the soundproof walls and excellent acoustics are well worth it as soon as a group can afford the price.

Amy describes a Jelly rehearsal: "Jesse and Fred bring in the music and lyrics in skeleton form. Then we work on it together. The three of us sit around the piano and say things like, 'This line stinks. How about this?' When it's right—wow!"

A three-hour practice session is minimum. "That's five or six days a week! Want to talk about overnight sensations?" Amy's freckle-sprinkled nose wrinkles up in a grin. "I love it!" she whoops. "The rehearsals, the gigs, all of it!" Then, turning abruptly serious, she says, "As crazy and whacked out as I am, I'm disciplined." Another whoop brings her to her feet, "Do you know how lucky I am? No amount of money, no house on the hills, no man, no Maserati could make me feel the way I do when Jelly's out there on the stage. Man, I'm lucky!"

=15=

On with the Song

You've peeked through the keyhole into the lives of thirteen different categories of singers. How much they have in common! Much more than the seven indispensable ingredients for success—the ability to sing in tune, a sense of rhythm, a quick mind and good memory, a good musical education, good health and stamina, tenacity, and talent—described at the beginning.

For instance, almost all the singers you met knew at an early age that when they grew up they would in some way sing for their supper. Without exception, every singer you met played at least one musical instrument, and played it rather well. Without exception, none of those you met were overnight successes. All learned their trade and worked their way up the ladder to get where they are.

So much in common! But one thing stands out above everything else. Perhaps it should be added as number eight to the seven indispensable ingredients for success! All love to sing for their supper.

And now, what about your career as a singer? Do you know which path seems most suitable for your voice, for your special abilities? Listed in the Appendix are names and addresses of organizations that can help you on your way. It's not too soon to get going! Write to them; one of the reasons for their existence is to be helpful to those who want to know more. For instance, if you write to the Country Music Association asking for whatever material they might have that would be of interest to a fledging songwriter, you will receive a booklet titled "What Every Songwriter Should Know," a two-page list of suggested books to read, plus a wealth of information about country music and the Country Music Association.

Many of the organizations listed put out regular publications. Reading them will give you a very good idea of what the business is all about. Write for a sample copy. Most are willing to send back issues, along with a request for subscription information. Some will put you on their mailing list for free.

And now—on with the song!

Appendix

Actors Equity Association
165 West 46th Street, New York, New York 10036

American Conservatory Theatre (ACT)
450 Geary Street, San Francisco, California 94102
For curriculum and enrollment information

American Educational Theatre Association, Inc.
726 Jackson Place N.W., Washington, D.C. 20566
For *The Directory of American College Theatre*, a listing of accredited institutions offering courses in musical and dramatic theater

American Federation of Television and Radio
Artists (AFTRA)
1350 Avenue of the Americas, New York, New York 10019
Labor organization covering performers in radio, TV, commercials and recordings

American Guild of Musical Artists (AGMA)
1841 Broadway, New York, New York 10019
National labor union covering professional entertainment in concert, recital, oratorio, opera, dance

American Guild of Variety Artists (AGVA)
1540 Broadway, New York, New York 10036
Represents performers in the night club, variety, circus, and allied fields

American Society of Composers, Authors, and Publishers (ASCAP)
1 Lincoln Plaza, New York, New York 10023
Performing rights society covering music writers and publishers

Association of Professional Sacred Singers
474 Brooklyn Avenue, Brooklyn, New York 11225

Broadcast Music, Inc. (BMI)
589 Fifth Avenue, New York, New York 10017
Publication: *BMI: The Many Worlds of Music*

Central Opera Service
Metropolitan Opera, Lincoln Center, New York, New York 10023
For career and awards brochures, listings of workshops and companies

Church Music Association of America
548 Lafond Avenue, St. Paul, Minnesota 55103
Publication: *Sacred Music*

Concert Artists Guild, Inc.
154 West 57th Street, Studio 136, New York, New York 10019
For information on auditions and awards

Country Music Association, Inc.
Seven Music Circle North, Nashville, Tennessee 37203
Publication: *CMA Close-Up*

Juilliard School of Theater Arts
Lincoln Center Plaza, New York, New York 10023
For enrollment and curriculum information

Musical Theater Workshop
135 North Grand Avenue, Suite 327, Los Angeles, California 90012
For enrollment and curriculum information

Music Educators National Conference (MENC)
1902 Association Drive, Reston, Virginia 22091
Publication: *Music Educators' Journal*

National Association for Music Therapy
P.O. Box 610, Lawrence, Kansas 66044
Publication: *Journal of Music Therapy*

National Association of Schools of Music
One Dupont Circle, NY Suite 650
Washington, D.C. 20036
For information on schools offering music curriculums

National Association of Teachers of Singing, Inc. (NATS)
250 West 57th Street, Suite 2129, New York,
New York 10019
For directory of membership, contest information
Publication: *The NATS Bulletin*

National Music Publishers Association
110 East 59th Street, New York, New York 10022
Publication: *NMPA Bulletin*

Show Business
136 West 44th Street, New York, New York 10036
For *Summer Theatre*, a yearly booklet that lists summer
theaters in the United States

Trade Papers—Records:

Billboard
900 Sunset Blvd., Los Angeles, California 90069 or
1 Astor Plaza, New York, New York 10036

Cashbox
6565 Sunset Blvd., Hollywood, California 90028 or
119 West 57th Street, New York, New York 10019

Record World
6290 Sunset Blvd., Hollywood, California 90028 or
1700 Broadway, New York, New York 10019

Trade Papers—Theatrical:

Show Business
136 West 44th Street, New York, New York 10036

Variety
154 West 46th Street, New York, New York 10036

Backstage
20 West 43rd Street, New York, New York 10036

Theatre Communications Group
20 West 43rd Street, New York, New York 10036
For list of nonprofit professional theaters

Theme Parks:
Penn Central Corporation—Six Flags
3 Penn Center Plaza, Philadelphia, Pennsylvania 19102

NLT Corporation—Opry Land
Nashville Life Center, Nashville, Tennessee 37250

Marriott Corporation
5161 River Road, Washington, D.C. 20016

Walt Disney Productions
500 South Buena Vista Street, Burbank, California 91521

Contact all for: Audition information